THE DANGEROUS JOURNEY

A boy's adventure in czarist Russia

THE DANGEROUS JOURNEY

Moshe Weinberg

TARGUM/FELDHEIM

First published 1999
Copyright © 1999 by Moshe Weinberg

All rights reserved

No part of this publication may be translated, reproduced, stored in a retrieval system, or transmitted in any form or by any means, electronic, mechanical, photocopying, recording, or otherwise, without prior permission in writing from both the copyright holder and the publisher.

Published by:
Targum Press, Inc.
22700 W. Eleven Mile Rd.
Southfield, MI 48034

Distributed by:
Feldheim Publishers
200 Airport Executive Park
Nanuet, NY 10954

Distributed in Israel by:
Targum Press Ltd.
POB 43170
Jerusalem 91430

Printed in Israel

DEDICATED TO

My wife
Rochelle, *shetichyeh*

Her dedication, encouragement, and support have always motivated me to achieve my goals and to pursue my career in *chinuch*. She herself is an excellent educator and a selfless mother. As a devoted partner, she had a major role in helping me complete this book.

My parents
Rabbi Shneur and Phyllis Weinberg, *sheyichyu*

I appreciate the lessons they continue to teach me about *chesed, mesirus nefesh, hachnasas orchim,* and their devotion to *chinuch*. I learned from them to strive for the impossible by using one's potential to its fullest. Their success as authors themselves inspired me to follow their example and write my own book.

DEDICATED TO

My children
Yudi, Mordechai, Avi, Meir, and Eli, *sheyichyu*

They provide us with much *nachas* and satisfaction. We are proud of their *middos*, their enthusiasm for learning Torah, and their own personal development.

My father-in-law,
Mr. Yechezkel Groner, *sheyichyeh*
and
in memory of my mother-in-law,
חיה ויטה בת ר' יהושע שלמה ע"ה

As Holocaust survivors, they suffered tremendous loss and upheaval. Yet, because of their strong determination, they overcame many obstacles, and they succeeded in reinstating all the religious values of their youth to their family. This personal lesson in *bitachon* in Hashem was meaningfully transmitted to all of us.

ACKNOWLEDGMENTS

I would like to thank

— Miss Sandra Pekar, who typed the rough draft, and Mrs. Leah Belfon, my very competent editor.

— All of my students, who awaited their daily installment of this story at the end of class each day. Their feedback helped me further develop the storyline, which was based on a short story in *Talks and Tales*.

— My publisher, Rabbi Dombey, and Shoshana Lepon and Suri Brand of Targum Press for their editing. Without their help this book could not have been published.

PROLOGUE

Dovid's excitement overwhelmed him as he stood waiting for his parents' carriage at the old station. They were coming home today! His parents never returned from a journey without bringing him and his sister, Devorah, some special gifts.

Their parents had gone away on important business, and, for the very first time, Devorah had looked after Dovid on her own. At seventeen, she was very capable, and Dovid, at fourteen, was quite mature for his age. The two of them shared a special closeness. They even looked alike. All the townspeople, even the non-Jews, knew they were brother and sister. They both had carrot-red, curly hair, quite unusual for the district, and were on the skinny side, though they ate whatever their mother served, and whatever she served was delicious.

Their mother fussed over them all the time, and she'd been hesitant to leave them on their own. "We'll do just fine by ourselves," Devorah had reassured her. "Don't worry about a thing! We're not little children any longer."

"Well, be sure to lock the house at night," warned their mother. "You know that Dovid's started walking around in his sleep. We don't want to lose him!"

Devorah had laughed and wrapped her arm protectively around Dovid's waist. Dovid knew his mother had been convinced. She trusted them, and he would not let her down.

As he stood impatiently in the station, waiting for his beloved parents, Dovid thought of the day of their departure. Only four days ago it was, and the memory was fresh in his mind.

With the coachman waiting, the children had watched their father help their mother into the carriage. How beautiful she had looked in her long blue dress! Her hat matched her dress exactly and had been made for her in Moscow the last time she was there. Indeed, she was elegant from head to toe! But the most beautiful of all was the smile that lit up her face. She was known for her unassuming acts of kindness — people often saw her leave baskets of food for the needy and drop envelopes full of rubles at doorsteps of people who were down on their luck. Everyone knew she was good as well as beautiful, and her noble character was reflected in her smile. That was the main thing, Dovid thought.

His father, too, was a refined and gracious man. He, too, was known for his humility and hospitality. And everybody marveled at his great scholarship and Torah learning.

When Dovid's parents left, his father had been simply

dressed, as always, but he looked very elegant in his traveling clothes. He was always perfectly groomed and immaculate. Dovid admired his confidence and dignity. One day, he hoped, he would be just like his father.

Now, any minute, his parents would be back. The large clock on the station wall had been there for as long as Dovid could remember, its black paint peeling off. The wallpaper, too, had seen better days. It had a pattern of dark brown trees against a muddy beige background. Some of the leaves were dropping from the trees, and it seemed to Dovid that the leaves, the trees — the whole business — should have been taken down a long time ago and replaced with something more modern. Worn wallpaper and peeling paint would never be allowed in his house, Dovid reflected. His parents would never put up with such shabbiness.

Still, Dovid like the atmosphere in the station. The old wooden benches were worn and rather uncomfortable, but nobody complained. The weight of the years had left their mark on everything, but travelers found it as cozy as their living room. A large iron stove in the center kept the small room warm. Every half-hour or so, Ivan, the stationmaster, would feed it chunks of sweet-smelling oak, and steam would sizzle from it. Dovid loved the sound of the steam and the crackle of the fire he could just glimpse inside the stove.

Though its paint was peeling, the old clock was still reliable. It was 3:45, and the carriage was due at 4:30. Dovid knew he was early, but wanted to make sure he'd be there when his parents arrived.

Dovid kept looking at the clock, watching the hands move slowly past the hour. Four, four-thirty, a quarter to five... By five there was still no carriage, and the people in the waiting room were starting to get restless. They chatted among themselves, wondering what had happened.

By six Dovid was nervous. Where was the coach? It was always on time.

At eight the people waiting at the station started leaving. Something must have happened to the carriage wheels, they said, or maybe a rainstorm was slowing the coachman down. The carriage could arrive soon, but there was a chance it wouldn't come till the morning. Better to just go home — there was dinner to cook and children to put to bed. Eventually Dovid, too, got up to leave.

That night, Dovid lay awake, unable to sleep. Where were his parents? Why hadn't they come home? Such a thing had never happened before. Devorah, too, had been frantic, but thought they would surely arrive in the morning.

Exhausted from worry, Dovid fell into a fitful sleep. The next morning he rose early. He rushed to his parents' room first thing, but their beds were empty.

When Dovid entered the kitchen, Devorah had breakfast waiting. The tea was hot, and the oatmeal was thick and drenched with sugar and cream, just the way he liked it. There was cheese and fruit on the table. Dovid felt like a king. He thanked his sister for the meal and thanked the Creator for his many blessings. When he finished eating, he set off for school.

On the way, he decided to make a detour and headed for the station to see if the carriage had arrived. It hadn't.

Dovid paced back and forth, thinking about what he should do next. He strolled up to Ivan, who was busy with paperwork. "Good morning to you," he said to the stationmaster respectfully. "Excuse me, please, when will the carriage arrive, the one that was expected yesterday afternoon?"

Ivan smiled at Dovid and replied, "I'm sorry, my dear boy. I really don't know. We're expecting two other passengers besides your parents and lots of packages, too. That's why so many people were waiting here yesterday. People are always anxious to get their packages!

"I can't understand what happened. Usually, when the carriage is late, someone comes on horseback and tells us why. We've never had to wait overnight. I'm going to have to send out a man on horseback to see what's happened. Some minor thing, for sure. Your parents will be here very soon. So run along to school now. If they see you're out of school, they won't be very happy!"

Dovid smiled. He had known Ivan all his life and really wanted to believe him. He went to school feeling much better.

It didn't take the rider who went to investigate long to discover the horrible truth. In the middle of the road lay the horses, still attached to the carriage, their bodies riddled with bullets. The coachman lay dead, face-down on the road. All four passengers had been shot, too. Robbery had obviously been the motive, for all the passengers' jewelry and wallets were gone. Gone, too, were the dozens of packages that the stationmaster and the townspeople had been expecting. With everyone dead, no one would be able to identify the robbers.

The townspeople were astounded. They had heard of stagecoach robberies, but such a tragedy had never happened so close to home.

Everyone was broken-hearted with grief, and their hearts went out to the bereaved families. They cried most for Devorah and Dovid, now orphans. Rabbi Silverberg, the town *rav*, broke the news to them.

Dovid could not believe what he was hearing. It seemed like a nightmare from which he could not awaken. For Devorah it was the same. A horrible sense of emptiness and loss overwhelmed them both.

"I can't cry," said Dovid, stone-faced. "I can't feel anything."

Devorah's grief, on the other hand, burst like a dam, and she wept uncontrollably.

"Cry, Dovid, cry," urged the rabbi softly. "Let it all out."

But Dovid's face was a mask, covering all the turmoil he felt inside.

Dovid is turning his heart into stone, the rabbi thought, *to survive the pain.*

THE GREAT CHANGE

Before tragedy struck the family, Dovid had been a very happy boy, who had loved his father and mother beyond belief. The family lived in a warm Jewish community in a little town in czarist Russia. The name of the town was Rukichki. It was in the province of Kovno, in Belarus, also known as White Russia.

Dovid was born during the reign of Alexander III, head of the House of Romanov and emperor of Russia. The czar was a powerful leader, and people lived and died according to his word.

Czar Alexander was a complex man. He opened up Russia to Western ideas, and the entire country prospered while he sat on the throne. But he ruled with a harsh hand and speedily put down any challenge to his authority. Anyone suspected of rebelling against him was instantly put to death, no questions asked.

Life wasn't so bad for the Jews under the czar, but it

wasn't so good, either. They were tolerated with varying degrees of benevolence, depending on the town. If the town's mayor was good, the Jews could live a normal life. If he wasn't, Heaven help them!

Dovid's town was blessed with a nice old mayor who had been there forever and never bothered anybody. Oleg Nikolaevitch left the Jews alone, and they, in turn, did whatever he wished. He wanted them to visit him on New Year's? Of course. He wanted a few delicacies from their shops and forgot to pay the bill? No problem. They looked the other way, and so did he. This arrangement worked out just fine for everyone.

Dovid enjoyed living in the town. He liked the mayor, too, and Oleg Nikolaevitch even knew his name. Dovid's father had been a very important man. He had been the one who spoke for the Jewish community whenever a delegation had to go to the mayor's house for something or another. Dovid thought of the time his father had taken him along, and the mayor had pinched his cheek and given him a ruble.

The mayor lived in a big house where lots of haughty servants walked about in fancy uniforms. The maids wore black dresses with white collars and cuffs and little frilly aprons — just like the French maids whose pictures Dovid had seen in books.

Dovid thought he heard snatches of French being spoken at the mayor's house. The Russian upper classes had taken on French as their second language. Wealthy Russian boys had French tutors who came to their homes. The sound of it was strange and oddly musical to Dovid's ears.

The servants' uniforms were like those of soldiers on parade. Their shoes were perfectly shined, as if impervious to the dust of the streets. These elegantly dressed men walked around serving the Jewish delegation pretty little drinks from silver trays. *How nice to be a mayor*, Dovid had thought, *and to have all these people wait on you. Maybe I, too, could be a mayor someday!*

Dovid had discussed this idea with his father on the way home. "No," his father said, laughing, as Dovid walked alongside him, holding his hand. "Being a mayor is not a job for a Jewish boy."

"Why not?" asked Dovid.

"Because," his father said with a sigh. "Just because."

Now Dovid was an orphan. He would never go anywhere with his father again. In one tragic instant he had lost everything, even the ability to feel.

Indeed, Dovid was surprised at what was going on inside his heart. Why wasn't he grieving more? He loved his parents. He missed them. But strangely, in a way he could not understand or attempt to explain, he felt detached. Like a limb broken off a tree. Deep down, Dovid knew he would never be the same. Sweet, beautiful, loving Dovid was gone.

After breaking the tragic news to Dovid, Rabbi Silverberg had put his arm around the boy's shoulder and took him and Devorah to his home. Rebbetzin Silverberg took them in as if they were her own, and in a way they were. The Silverbergs had known Devorah and Dovid from birth.

Rabbi Silverberg had been the *sandak* at Dovid's bris. He had held him lovingly while the *mohel* circumcised him. He and Rebbetzin Silverberg had participated in all their family *simchah*s.

Both plump and soft, they had kind, caring faces. They looked more like brother and sister than husband and wife. They were both quite short and waddled slightly when they walked.

It was the Silverbergs' intention that Devorah and Dovid remain with them. All their children were married, with children of their own, all living in other towns. It would be nice to have children in the house again. They would raise the two orphans and help them get married and start their own homes. They hoped their home would give Devorah and Dovid some comfort.

But in less than a week another tragedy struck. The Creator of the universe decides who will be born and who will die, and when. The power to understand where, when, or why is not ours.

Rabbi and Mrs. Silverberg's home became a *shivah* house yet again. Their daughter Rifkah's husband, a blacksmith in a town only five hours away, suffered fatal burns in an accident in his shop. Accompanied by a large group of friends, a weeping Rifkah, her young daughter Sarah, and her twin babies made their way in a long caravan to her parents' house. They had come to stay, and so other plans would have to be made for Dovid and Devorah. As much as the Silverbergs wanted to keep them, there simply wasn't enough room.

Devorah could go to live with an aunt and uncle in another town. They had no children, and the aunt was sick. They would look after Devorah, and the girl would take care of her aunt.

But they could not take Dovid, too. He was a young boy who still needed care, and his aunt and uncle were not up to the job. Unfortunately, their town was far away — three days' journey by carriage — so Devorah and Dovid would see one another very rarely.

How sad, Dovid thought, *that we should have to be separated.* But there was no help for it, and before he knew it, Devorah was gone.

The townspeople met in the shul, where they always met, in good times and bad, to decide how to best care for Dovid. Most of the townspeople were very poor. Their homes were already too small for their large families. None of them could afford to take in Dovid as their own child, so a creative solution had to be found. What they finally decided wasn't the best solution, but under the circumstances it would have to do.

Dovid would spend one month a year in each of twelve homes. He would always have a place to live, and no family would be obliged to support him for the entire year.

The rabbi presented the idea to Dovid one day after school. Dovid had mixed feelings about it. On the one hand, he loved Rabbi and Mrs. Silverberg and didn't want to leave them. On the other hand, he didn't have a minute's quiet to study or sleep because of the presence of Rifkah and her children.

"I'll do it. I'm sure I'll be very happy," said Dovid to the rabbi. But inside, his heart sank. He would never have a place to call his own, a true home. From now on, he would have to take care of himself.

The first home Dovid went to was his aunt Sarah's. She and his uncle Yonah adored him and very much wanted him to stay permanently. But Aunt Sarah and Uncle Yonah had only two rooms and five children of their own. While he was there, Dovid made himself comfortable and was happy to have his cousins for company.

Dovid was a very good student, and often his aunt would say to his cousin, "Daniel, why can't you be more like Dovid? Dovid does his homework as soon as he comes home. Dovid is always ready for school on time. Dovid makes his bed without being reminded. Why can't you behave more like him?"

Daniel didn't like any of this one bit, but he accepted it because he loved Dovid like a brother.

For Dovid, staying with Aunt Sarah and Uncle Yonah would be remembered as a very pleasant time. As hard as it was for Dovid to put behind him the tragedy he had suffered and get on with his life, at least he was in a place where he was loved and wanted.

Though Dovid's aunt and uncle were very poor, there was one valuable item in the house: Aunt Sarah's silver candlesticks, which had been passed down to her by her grandmother, to whom she had been very close. Every Friday, Aunt Sarah polished those candlesticks until they gleamed.

The Great Change

As she recited the *berachah* over the Shabbos candles every week, Aunt Sarah always felt great joy. The beauty of those candlesticks and Aunt Sarah's glowing smile shone throughout the house. The candles cast a spell on everyone present, lifting up their hearts to welcome the Sabbath Queen.

On the third *erev Shabbos* that Dovid was at his aunt's house, she went to the cabinet to take out the candlesticks for their weekly polish. But instead of two beautiful silver candlesticks standing straight and tall in their cupboard, she found an empty shelf.

"Yonah," she cried, "the candlesticks are gone!"

Her husband, on his way out to shul for morning prayers, stopped in his tracks, horrified.

"Where could you have put them, Sarah? It's not like you to lose something, especially not your grandmother's candlesticks! I have to leave right now, but wake up the children to help you look for them."

As he left, Uncle Yonah sighed. *The candlesticks will surely be found*, he thought.

Aunt Sarah couldn't believe the candlesticks were lost. She had kept them in the same place for the past ten years. Every Friday morning she took them out, polished them, and placed them on the table. After Shabbos was over, she would clean them and put them back in the cabinet. What could have happened to them?

All the children, including Dovid, helped her search the house, but the precious candlesticks could not be found. Dovid's aunt was so upset that she sat down and cried.

Dovid's month with Uncle Yonah and Aunt Sarah soon ended, and he moved to the home of Mr. and Mrs. Green. The Greens were lovely people. Although Dovid was sad to leave his cousins, he was not unhappy about moving to the Greens. They had three children, and one was was in Dovid's class.

Now Reuven and I will be even closer, thought Dovid. *We'll be like brothers.*

Reuven was very happy, because he was the only boy in the Green family. Now he and Dovid would be equally matched against the girls. Reuven chuckled to himself, thinking of all the pranks he and Dovid would play on his unsuspecting sisters!

The two boys had a great time together. They became inseparable, at school as well as at home. They did their homework together and played together every chance they got. They went for long walks every Shabbos and had little picnics in the nearby forest during the week. Sometimes they did their homework there. They had found the perfect place — a clearing surrounded by beautiful spring flowers and the song of birds. It was a very special time for both boys, and Dovid adjusted easily to the family routines.

While living in the Greens' home, Dovid also worked hard at his studies. And Mrs. Green would say the same thing to Reuven as his aunt Sarah had said to Daniel: "Reuven, why don't you study as hard as Dovid? Why aren't your grades as good as his? Why can't you be more like him?"

The Great Change

Time passed quickly at the Greens' house, and before Dovid realized it, his month with them was almost over. Before he moved on, though, another strange thing happened.

Although their house was small and sparsely furnished, one item brought the Greens a great deal of pride. Once, long ago, when they had managed to save up a small amount of money, Mr. Green had purchased a beautiful silver mezuzah case. Mr. Green had reasoned, "If it's for a mitzvah, we'll find the money." The Greens placed this special mezuzah case at the front entrance of their small home. People who passed by noticed its unusual beauty and would stop to kiss it, according to the tradition.

Mr. Green woke up one morning and got ready to go to shul. As usual, without even thinking about what he was doing, he lifted his hand to touch the mezuzah at the front door. To Mr. Green's profound shock, his hand brushed against bare wood. What could have happened to the treasured mezuzah? Had it fallen? He looked on the ground, but found nothing. Mr. Green went inside to ask his family if they had any idea where it was. It was early morning, and everyone was still asleep, but Mr. Green could not let this wait. The mystery had to be solved.

First he woke his wife. "Shaindel," he said, his voice breaking, "have you seen the mezuzah?" He did not have to say which mezuzah. She knew immediately which one he was talking about. Shaindel Green looked at her husband in astonishment. "What do you mean, Meir? The mezuzah is on the front door. Where else would it be?"

Mr. Green explained. Mrs. Green got up immediately to help him. They went to each of the children, and of course Dovid, to see if any of them knew anything about the missing mezuzah. They had all seen it on the doorpost the night before. "Where else would it be?" they asked, echoing their mother when she had been woken up.

Mr. Green had no idea what to do next. He headed to shul to daven as usual, and from there he went to work. But he could not get his mind off the missing mezuzah. All day Mr. Green kept thinking about where it might be. It was the only precious object in his house.

Several days passed, but there was no sign of it. The family finally accepted that it was gone — either stolen or somehow misplaced. It was unlikely they would ever see it again.

Soon afterwards, it was time for Dovid to leave the Greens. He was upset about leaving, for he had become accustomed to their home and had become deeply attached to their son, Reuven. But Dovid knew he had to go. The good news was that he was going to the home of Mr. and Mrs. Katz.

The Katzes had no children. Because of this they were, in a way, like parents to everybody else's children. Mr. Katz in particular was known as a man who adored children, and everybody knew that if Mr. Katz was around, a small piece of candy or some other treat would soon be coming their way.

When Dovid arrived, Mr. and Mrs. Katz did everything they could to help him settle in and make him feel at home.

They lived in a very small house, with only one room, so Dovid had to sleep on a mat on the floor. It wasn't the best arrangement, but Mr. and Mrs. Katz made Dovid feel truly welcome.

For his part, Dovid tried to be a good guest. Every morning he folded up his mat neatly and put it away. He also did many chores for the Katzes. He cut the wood and brought it inside every day. And since he was up early, he always lit the fire so the house was warm when the Katzes awoke. Often he had the kettle boiling for tea by the time they woke up. After the evening meal, Dovid cleared the table and helped Mrs. Katz wash the dishes.

Dovid loved the evenings he spent with the Katzes in their home. His host was an excellent conversationalist who liked to twirl his black moustache to emphasize a point. He used his hands a lot when he talked and used up so much energy that he always stayed thin, no matter what he ate.

Mrs. Katz was on the heavy side. She liked to take a rest whenever she could. "I think I'll retire to the couch," she'd say after every meal. That was Dovid and Mr. Katz's signal to get up and clear away the dishes.

Both Mr. and Mrs. Katz were very entertaining and had many tales to tell about the good old days. Dovid learned a lot about the history of the town and its people, who was related to whom through marriage, and a lot of other interesting things. Mrs. Katz told lots of funny stories about engagements and weddings, and Mr. Katz made Dovid laugh with his many jokes. Both of them gave Dovid lots of attention, and he listened in awe to their marvelous stories. Dovid was impressed that, although both Mr. and Mrs. Katz were great talkers, they never said one word of *lashon hara*.

A couple of weeks after Dovid had settled in, Mr. Katz stopped at a small kiosk for a cup of tea on his way to work. He'd stop there sometimes after shul for a quick drink and a little chat with the owner, his lifelong friend. On that particular day he reached into his pocket for some loose change to pay for the tea, but his hand came out empty. There was not a single coin in his pocket.

Mr. Katz was surprised. He was sure that the evening before he had received a handful of change while grocery shopping. As always, he'd put the coins into the pocket of his pants. It seemed strange that his pocket was empty now.

That evening, while Dovid washed the dishes, Mr. Katz quietly asked his wife if she'd taken the change from his pocket and forgotten to mention it to him. No, Mrs. Katz replied. She hadn't spent any money that day at all. She had no idea where the money could have gone.

The matter of the missing change greatly bothered Mr. Katz. He was very organized and seldom lost anything. But Mr. Katz had many other things on his mind, and the incident was quickly forgotten.

SUSPICIONS AROUSED

Aunt Sarah, Mrs. Green, and Mrs. Katz were old friends — they had known each other all their lives. So when they happened to be shopping at the same time, as they were one afternoon the next week, it was a great chance for them to catch up with one another's news.

As they piled their wagons with groceries, Aunt Sarah joked, "Why are you buying so much food, Rochel? I know you love your food, but how much can the two of you eat?"

Mrs. Katz laughed. "Oh no, my dear Sarah! All this food's not for me! We have a very important guest at our house now — your nephew. He's a fine boy with a fine appetite, I'm happy to say."

Then Mrs. Katz's tone suddenly changed, and a tear ran down her plump cheek. "We all must look after him now that his parents are gone." Dovid's mother had been one of her very best friends.

Shaindel Green remarked that only last month Dovid had been a guest at her home, and she, too, mentioned how much she and her husband had enjoyed their time with him. In fact, she said, they were looking forward to having him again when their turn came around next year.

Sarah mentioned that she and her husband had hosted Dovid the month before Mrs. Green. "He left right about the time my grandmother's silver candlesticks disappeared."

"You know," explained Mrs. Green, "we've also lost our most precious possession! It took years to save up for that silver mezuzah case, and now it's gone."

"Well, we never found those candlesticks. It's been two months!"

The other women were surprised and asked Sarah how such a thing could possibly happen. Didn't she always keep them in the same cabinet?

"Yes, of course," Sarah replied. "But when I went to the cupboard to take them out that *erev Shabbos*, they were nowhere to be found. It was as if they'd disappeared into thin air."

"That's funny," said Mrs. Katz. "My husband was missing some change from his pocket just the other day. He was quite upset by it. You know how careful he is about everything."

It was an odd coincidence. Each of them had experienced a loss one after the other. First the missing candlesticks. Then the silver mezuzah case. Then Mr. Katz's money.

Slowly the women's eyes met. Each had reached the same conclusion. Every time an item had gone missing, Dovid had been a guest in that house. The shock of this realization was so great that none of them could speak. They didn't have to; each knew what the others were thinking. How could they suspect the boy of such awful deeds? Yet, in their hearts, all three believed he was the culprit. Who else would have had the opportunity? The three friends quickly said their goodbyes and went their separate ways.

Mrs. Katz was particularly upset. She went straight home and waited impatiently for her husband to return from work. When Mr. Katz finally arrived, his wife told him about the conversation in the grocery store. Mr. Katz had nearly forgotten about the money that had gone missing from his pocket, but now he felt he must find out if there was any truth to the terrible allegations. He didn't want to be hasty, though. If they were wrong, Dovid would be terribly insulted. After the loss of his parents he needed friends, and false accusations would only push him away.

That evening, Mr. Katz deliberately left some coins in his pants pocket. If they were still there in the morning, they'd know Dovid was innocent. All night Mr. Katz tossed and turned. He couldn't help wondering if the coins he'd left in his pants pocket would be there in the morning. As soon as he woke up, he went to check. He stuck his hand into the pocket, but withdrew it empty-handed. The money was gone! Mr. Katz's heart was racing. Besides himself, the only other people in the house were his wife and his invited guest, Dovid.

Still, Mr. Katz did not want to judge Dovid unfavorably. Perhaps his wife, worried about possible theft, had removed the coins. Before reaching any hasty conclusions, he questioned his wife. She had gone shopping only the day before, she replied, and had no need for the money and had been nowhere near his pants. Tragically, the evidence was all too clear that Dovid was a thief.

At shul, Mr. Katz, who was careful never to speak negatively about others, sadly informed the other men that Dovid was a thief.

Everyone knew that the tragedy of his parents' death had hit Dovid very hard. They felt sympathetic toward him and could not accept Mr. Katz's accusations. "It's *lashon hara*. You can't go around saying bad things about other people."

But after Mr. Katz told them the whole story, they had to believe that Dovid was not the boy he seemed to be.

Mr. Katz, warm, wonderful Mr. Katz, proposed that Dovid be thrown out of town and that he no longer be allowed in any of their homes. Yes, he was an orphan, a Jew in need of *chesed*, but how can a person let a robber stay in his home? To do so is nothing but an invitation to steal!

Many of the men came around to Mr. Katz's point of view. What he was saying was perfectly logical, and there didn't seem to be any other explanation. But Rabbi Silverberg would not hear of it.

The rabbi was a wise man who had led the community for over twenty-five years. In all that time he had never taken a salary from the townspeople, though he wasn't rich by any means. Many of his congregants insisted on bringing him and his *rebbetzin* food and other useful items. He accepted the small presents in order not to insult the givers. The townspeople loved and respected the rabbi. His opinion carried lots of weight, and everyone turned to him when they needed the answers to tough questions.

Now the men listened closely to what the rabbi had to say. He reminded them of the halachah that a person could not be accused of a crime based on circumstantial evidence. Before ruling on the matter, the rabbi proposed a test that would clearly indicate whether Dovid was indeed a robber.

Rabbi Silverberg told Mr. Katz to take home a valuable item and present it to his wife as a birthday gift. It did not matter that it wasn't Mrs. Katz's birthday. Mr. Katz was to make it quite obvious to both his wife and Dovid where he was putting this item. After that, he was to keep his eye on Dovid and see if it disappeared or remained where he'd left it.

The people of the shul agreed that this was a fair way to decide the issue, and Mr. Katz was given a silver letter opener to offer his wife. Before going to work, Mr. Katz rushed home to tell his wife about the plans so she would know what was happening.

That evening, as soon as Mr. Katz walked in the door, he called out loudly to his wife, "Happy birthday, my dear

Rochel. I've brought you a small gift." Dovid, who was sitting at the table doing his homework, could not help but overhear.

"Oh, thank you so much!" exclaimed Mrs. Katz. She unwrapped the gift and appeared to be delighted with the silver letter opener. She thanked her husband profusely and called Dovid over to see it.

Mr. Katz held his gift up to the light and said to Dovid, "Look at this wonderful silver letter opener." He stressed the word *silver*. When Mr. Katz was sure that Dovid understood the value of the gift, he commented casually, "Well, I think the cupboard would be a good place to keep it." He made sure Dovid was watching when he put it away. Feeling sick inside, Mr. Katz noted Dovid's obvious interest in where he was placing the letter opener.

Night fell and bedtime preparations began. Mr. Katz wished Dovid a good night and retired behind the curtain which hung across the room, where he and Mrs. Katz slept. He was glad his wife had left town to visit her mother. She was staying overnight so she wouldn't have to travel in the dark.

Mr. Katz heard Dovid walk toward the mat where he always slept. Mr. Katz, however, did not plan to sleep. After he felt sure that Dovid was asleep, he got up and stood behind the floor-length curtain. That would be the best way to observe anything that might occur, thought Mr. Katz.

By eleven o'clock, Mr. Katz was feeling drowsy. It was very hard for him, after putting in a full day's work, to stand

and wait behind the curtain. He yearned for sleep, yet forced himself to remain there. He had to know — the question of Dovid's guilt was weighing on his mind.

Twelve o'clock came and went. Then it was one. At 1:30 Mr. Katz, who had been dozing fitfully behind the curtain, suddenly awoke with a start. He could hear noises in the room. Holding his breath so he wouldn't be heard, he peeked out from the curtain and waited silently to see what would happen.

Sure enough, Dovid was awake, walking around the room. He was heading toward the cupboards which were nailed to the wall on the other side of the room, near the ice box where the food was kept. Still, Mr. Katz had no proof that anything was amiss. Maybe Dovid just wanted a midnight snack or a drink of water.

He would have to follow Dovid to find out what the boy was up to. Mr. Katz slipped out from behind the curtain, and as Dovid approached the cupboards, Mr. Katz was only a few steps behind him. If Dovid had turned around at that point, the boy would have been very surprised. But Dovid was focused on what he was doing.

Mr. Katz's heart sank. Dovid wasn't going to fix himself a snack. He wasn't going to take a drink of water. Dovid had stopped directly in front of the cupboard where the silver letter opener lay. Even now Mr. Katz hoped Dovid was heading for the cookie jar on top of the ice box. Dovid loved those cookies, and they had told him he could have as many as he liked.

Mr. Katz watched silently as Dovid stretched out his hand. He could barely stop himself from shouting, "No, Dovid, don't take the letter opener! You're not a thief! You're a good Jewish boy!"

But, despite the turmoil he felt inside, Mr. Katz kept quiet. He knew Rabbi Silverberg was right. He had to allow the scene to unfold and report to the rabbi and the members of the shul afterwards.

Dovid opened the cupboard. He took out the letter opener and slipped it under his pajama top. Then he quickly headed back to his room. Never once did he turn around.

Mr. Katz watched as Dovid opened his trunk and put the letter opener inside. Then Dovid locked the trunk and climbed back into bed.

When Mr. Katz was sure that Dovid was asleep, he, too, made his way to bed. But he stayed awake all night, staring at the ceiling. He would have only bad news to share when he went to shul in the morning.

BAD NEWS

Mr. Katz was one of the last of the congregation to arrive at shul and had only enough time to put on his tallis before the davening began. He prayed with all his heart for Dovid, the orphan boy, not knowing what would become of him, yet fully aware that he could not remain among the people who had taken him in as their own.

At the end of davening, everyone sat down and waited for Mr. Katz to speak. "Dovid took the letter opener," Mr. Katz told them in a trembling voice. "As much as we love him, we cannot let him stay. He has to go."

The men were silent, unwilling to believe. Could their Dovid really be a thief?

"He has to go," repeated Mr. Katz. "There is no other way."

Mr. Katz turned to the man whom everyone respected. "Rabbi," he said, "I've done all you asked. We tested Dovid and he failed."

Rabbi Silverberg stood up. He looked around the room and met everyone's eyes. Then he turned to Mr. Katz. "It would seem that you're right, that Dovid is a thief. But don't forget the tragedy that has befallen him. Let's remember his age and that every person, including every one of us, has sinned before.

"Is there no such thing as forgiveness?" the rabbi continued. "Is there no such thing as *teshuvah*? Why not give Dovid a chance? Maybe he'll admit to what he's done and offer to return the stolen objects.

"Every day in Shemoneh Esreh we pray to Hashem to give us the chance to do *teshuvah*. We beg Him to listen when we tell him we want to improve. Dovid should also be given this chance."

Many of the men nodded in agreement. But many more had angry expressions on their faces.

Slowly Mr. Katz rose. "Rabbi Silverberg," he said with a touch of annoyance, "enough of these games. We wouldn't allow a snake in our homes. We can't allow a thief, either."

The rabbi replied, "I'm willing to confront Dovid right now and ask him what happened. Let him tell me why he's done these awful things. I'm sure he'll feel very bad and say he's sorry. In such a case, we must certainly forgive him."

Mr. Katz sighed. "Rabbi, I suggest we have a secret vote. If it's not a clear matter of Jewish law, majority rules!"

"All right," agreed Rabbi Silverberg, suddenly feeling very old and very tired.

The shammas went to find a pen and paper for the vote.

As was the custom, the rabbi would vote only if there was a tie. After everyone wrote down his choice, the ballots were collected, and the shammas slowly counted the votes.

The room was absolutely silent. Rabbi Silverberg was conscious of his own breathing, his own heartbeat. He felt that everyone in the room could hear his heart pounding.

The silence hung like a bad dream in the air as the shammas counted the votes. He did it three times just to be sure. Then he, too, looked around the room. The others looked at him expectantly, waiting to hear the results.

Mr. Katz wanted to be wrong. He wanted this to be just another nightmare from which he would soon awaken. He wanted to rise from his bed and find the letter opener just where he'd left it. But Mr. Katz was not in his bed. He was sitting in shul with his rabbi and his friends, and Dovid was on trial for what Mr. Katz knew was his very life.

"It's a tie," the shammas said in a low voice. "Twenty-six for and twenty-six against."

Now it was up to the rabbi, and he was grateful Dovid would be given another chance. "It seems that a lot of people agree with me," he said, weighing his words carefully. "We must give Dovid another chance and see if he is willing to work with us. I'll go over right now and speak to him. Please wait for me and go to work a little later. I'll come right back and give you a report." Rabbi Silverberg didn't wait for their response. He simply turned around and left.

Some of the men went out for breakfast; others went to take care of business matters. The rest decided to stay in shul and learn Torah while they waited for the rabbi to return. But they all agreed, the sooner this matter was settled, the better. It could not be put off one more day.

Rabbi Silverberg walked quickly toward the Katz house. He remembered that Mrs. Katz was out of town. *Good*, thought the rabbi, *she doesn't need this!* Although the distance to the house was short, it seemed the longest journey of his life.

He knocked on the door, but there was no reply. He knocked again. Still nothing. The rabbi waited, and then began pounding on the door more insistently.

He heard Dovid's sleepy voice: "Who is it?"

The rabbi surprised himself with the strength of his own voice. "It's Rabbi Silverberg. I'm here to speak to you. Please open the door."

Dovid did not open the door. "Rabbi," he said, "could you come back in an hour, please, when I'm up and ready to receive you properly? I'm not even dressed."

"I'm sorry, Dovid, but I must speak to you at once. Open the door immediately!"

Slowly Dovid opened the door. "Come in," he said. "How can I help you?"

The rabbi's gaze penetrated Dovid's heart. He gestured to Dovid to sit down and took a chair opposite the boy.

"It's not how you can help me, but how I can help you," said the rabbi when they were seated. "Is there something you'd like to tell me, perhaps? Something you'd like to share before we go any further?"

Dovid stared at the rabbi. "Now you're really talking in riddles. What can you help me with? You've already done so much for me, Rabbi. How could I possibly ask for anything more?"

Rabbi Silverberg saw this would not be simple. "Dovid, are you sure there's nothing you'd like to say to me? Are you sure there's nothing you've done that you realize might be wrong? I'm here to help you!"

Dovid looked confused. "You're a Jewish boy, Dovid, continued the rabbi. "You know all about the concept of *teshuvah*. You also know that if a person confesses his sin and promises to improve in the future, he will be forgiven. Please, Dovid, don't make me say anymore."

When Dovid spoke, his voice was hard. "Rabbi Silverberg," he declared, "I have no idea what you're talking about. I try to do *teshuvah* whenever I do something wrong. Why are you asking me these questions?"

"Open your trunk, Dovid. There's something in it I would like to see."

"Rabbi, if you must look inside my trunk, then go ahead. I have nothing to hide. But why would you want to? My clothing is neat." When he saw the rabbi would not relent, he sighed. "All right, if you insist, I'll gladly open it for you."

Dovid walked over to his trunk and opened it. On top lay the letter opener.

Dovid's face turned red. "Now I understand everything," he cried. "You're accusing me of stealing this knife!

That's what this is all about! This is the knife Mr. Katz gave his wife as a birthday present. I have no idea how it got inside my trunk. I certainly didn't put it there!

"Somebody's trying to trick you, Rabbi! They put the knife there to ruin my reputation. I swear to you, Rabbi, I would never do such a thing!" Dovid sat down with his head in his hands and sobbed uncontrollably.

The rabbi hadn't expected this. Dovid continued to deny the theft even after being caught red-handed.

Rabbi Silverberg decided to give it one last try. "Dovid, please," he urged. "Enough of this. Admit to what you've done. Say you're sorry and you'll never do it again. If you don't, do you have any idea what's going to happen?"

Dovid stared at the rabbi. "I'm not a robber! I didn't take the letter opener! I have no idea how it got into my trunk. Someone close to you is trying to frame me for something I didn't do. And I don't know why!" Dovid's face was red, and his body shook.

The rabbi left the house and headed back to shul. He took much longer than usual, for a most distasteful task lay ahead of him. Never before had he felt such reluctance to face his congregants. But what had to be said had to be said. And as the rabbi, it was his job to say it.

He faced a solemn crowd. There was nothing the rabbi could say to lessen the pain they all felt. They felt for Dovid, they felt for the *neshamos* of his parents, but, most of all, they felt for themselves. They could not risk having such a person in their midst. The explanation Dovid had offered the rabbi, that someone was framing him, was beyond belief.

When the rabbi finished speaking, Mr. Katz rose. "Gentlemen," he said, weighing his words, "the matter is now tragically clear. I say Dovid must leave. He doesn't belong here."

The rabbi stood up. "Listen to me," he begged. "Remember what Dovid has been through. He doesn't even have his sister to turn to. The tragedy has obviously affected his mind to the point where he can no longer be held responsible for his actions. There has to be some way we can help him. If we throw him out, what will happen to him?"

"Fine," Mr. Katz spoke up quickly. "Let's put it to another vote."

But before the shammas could even bring in fresh paper, a young boy ran into the shul. He exclaimed breathlessly, "I just saw Dovid running away from town! He was screaming, 'I'm innocent! I'm not a robber! I'm innocent! How dare they do this to me? I'll be back, and I'll have my revenge. You'll all be sorry! Every last one of you!' "

The men were shocked. One by one they stood up and headed for work, deeply saddened at what had come to pass.

Why did things happen the way they did? It's hard to say. But one thing was for sure: Dovid had run away from his problem rather than face it.

Rabbi Silverberg took the blame. He should have spent more time with Dovid after his parents died. He should have worked harder to convince his congregants to have more sympathy for Dovid. He should have done more to help Dovid deal with his grief. Unfortunately, now it was too late.

Time passed, and gradually people put Dovid out of their minds. Not a word was heard of him, and no one mentioned his name.

A short while after Dovid's departure, a Russian peddler selling pots and pans passed through the town. As he chatted with a group of Jewish customers, he said something that immediately piqued everybody's interest.

"There was a skinny red-haired boy I saw begging a while back. He was the youngest beggar I've ever run into. But the strange part is," the peddler remarked, "the boy was wearing one of those black head coverings you all wear. To tell you the truth, I've never seen a Jew begging. Don't you guys always look after each other?"

The people looked at one another in shame. Who else could it have been but Dovid? He was skinny. He had red hair. The poor boy had run away and was now begging by the roadside.

EXILE

When Dovid left Rukichki, he walked for many hours, tired and hungry, unsure of where he'd spend the night. At the first town he came to, he asked how to get to the nearest inn. He was led to large gray building at the edge of the forest. Dovid didn't like the look of it, but he had to sleep somewhere. He was devastated when he found out how much a night at the inn would cost. It was so much!

Dovid had no choice but to sleep by the side of the road. He needed to hold on to the little money he had to buy food. That evening, his bed was a small hill of grass, with his arm as a pillow.

The next morning, Dovid found that he had shared the roadside with a fellow traveler. The man, who was still asleep, was in far worse shape than Dovid. His clothing was tattered, and his bones seemed to protrude from his body. David sat, staring at him, waiting for the man to awaken.

When he did, the man didn't seem too surprised to see Dovid there.

"My name's Peter," said the man. "What do you call yourself?"

Dovid had to think fast. His was a Jewish name, given at his bris milah, the name he lived by as a Jew. But now Dovid was in the outside world and would have to pick a name to suit. *What sounds like Dovid? I need a good Russian name,* he thought.

"My name's Dimitri," Dovid finally replied. "Do you live around here?"

Peter answered with a smile. "I live here, I live there, I live everywhere. I find food wherever I can. I sleep wherever I am."

"Sounds like a strange way to live," Dovid said.

"I don't have much of a choice. I have no money, no friends or relatives. My parents are long gone. This is the only way I can survive.

"I stand at the side of the road and beg. Some days I actually eat quite well if enough people feel sorry for me. Other days, when the pickings are slim, I don't get much food at all.

"It's not such a bad life. I meet other beggars, and we keep each other company. Sometimes we have a drink of wine together. As long as the weather isn't too cold, I'm okay."

It occurred to Dovid that perhaps this man could help him. If he was to survive, he'd have to learn how to be a good beggar.

Peter was more than happy to oblige. "Dimitri, if you

want to learn how to beg, just watch me. If I find a place to sleep, sleep right alongside me. If I find a good spot where people are generous, I'll let you sit down next to me. In fact, since most people have a soft spot for children, you could easily make a lot of money."

Eager to get some more money, Dovid sat down next to Peter and watched him carefully. Whenever someone passed by, Peter would yell out, "Please, a penny, a nickel, a piece of bread. I'm hungry! Can anybody help?" Most people ignored him, but every once in a while a kindly soul would throw him a coin or two or perhaps give him a little food. It all added up, and by lunch hour Peter and Dovid had more than enough money to buy themselves a loaf of bread, a drink, and a hunk of cheese.

Dovid didn't want to live like this for the rest of his life. But for now, it would have to do.

Dovid followed Peter for close to two weeks. Begging was difficult, but Dovid wasn't starving and he was learning how to manage on his own. Of course, his clothing was dirty and worn, and he was beginning to think that wearing a *kippah* and *tzitzis* was not helping him collect much money. He noticed that many people threw coins to Peter, but when they saw that Dovid was Jewish, they turned away.

Peter often told him to take off his *kippah* and tuck his *tzitzis* inside his pants. "People around here don't like Jews very much," Peter told him frankly. "Forget about being Jewish. The Jews in your community weren't very nice to you anyway."

Dovid didn't like what Peter was saying, but there was a lot of truth in it. After a few days of begging with no profit, Dovid took off his *kippah* and *tzitzis*. He was still a Jew, he reasoned, but he didn't have to wear those things in order to be Jewish.

Dovid also didn't daven anymore — he couldn't remember all the prayers. And he certainly couldn't think about keeping kosher.

After a few days of begging bareheaded, Dovid believed he had made the right decision. He was beginning to get quite good. Some days he brought in more money than Peter.

FARM LIFE

Dovid and Peter had been together for about a month, when a man walked over to Peter, drew him aside, and had a long conversation with him.

"Great news," Peter said to Dovid as soon as the man left. "Old man Boris is hiring workers again. That was his hired man who just came by. Every year at this time he takes on twenty or thirty people to help him pick his potatoes. The job doesn't last long, but we do get paid. We get three good meals and a roof over our heads. It's a nice change from begging. I always join his work force, and this year he wants me again.

"I think, Dimitri, that if I put in a good word for you, Boris will hire you, too. Are you interested?"

Dovid didn't know what to say. He had never picked potatoes in his life. But he didn't want to lose his good friend Peter. He wasn't sure how he'd manage without the older fellow, so he agreed.

The next day, Peter got up early and headed off to old man Boris's farm. The farmer recognized him and gladly welcomed him back. Peter knew this was a good moment to ask for a favor.

"Boris," he said in a confidential tone, "you've known me many years. I'm a serious worker, and I've never missed a day. I have a young friend who has no money, and I think he'd do good work for you. Would you give him a chance?"

Old man Boris was in a good mood that day and quickly agreed. Dovid and Peter were both to report to the farm the following morning. Peter told Dovid exactly what to expect. "We work six days a week and play on the seventh. On Sunday we go into town and have a great time," said Peter, relishing the memory of the previous year. "We drink beer and whiskey and come back ready to work another week."

All this sounded rather dismal to Dovid. He realized he'd have to work on Shabbos. Being bareheaded was one thing, but being *mechalel Shabbos*? Still, it was either that or starve. Later on, when he'd earned some money, he could quit and wouldn't have to work on Shabbos anymore. *Surely Hashem will understand,* he thought. *Hashem wouldn't want me to die from hunger.*

When the two of them reached the farm, old man Boris immediately motioned Dovid over. While Peter went right to work, Boris asked Dovid some questions. "What's your name, boy?"

"My name is Dimitri."

"You're a little young to be working in the fields. In fact, you're a little young to be a beggar. Where are you from? Where's your family?"

Dovid told the truth. "I'm from Rukichki, but my parents are dead. I have no home. I don't have anywhere to go."

Old man Boris persisted, "Don't you have any relatives or friends to look after you? Why weren't you sent to the church orphanage that the nuns of Rukichki run?"

Dovid answered softly, "I'm all alone in the world. My only friend is Peter. I'll work hard for you, sir. I really need the money. Please take me on. I promise you won't be sorry."

Old man Boris had a strange look on his face, a look Dovid didn't like. Although he had spoken to him nicely, there was something harsh about the man. The farmer was well over sixty, but he had the strength of a much younger man. He was tall and thin with thick gray hair and light-colored blue eyes that seemed to have no warmth. There was a coldness coming from him that Dovid had never felt from anyone before.

"You're Jewish, aren't you?" the old man said slowly. "A Jewish boy with no one in the world to care for him." His eyes glittered.

Suddenly afraid, Dovid said nothing. When he saw Dovid wasn't going to answer, old man Boris told Dovid to follow him. They walked through the fields in the blazing sun and soon arrived at a small hut. It was furnished with only a rickety cot and a table and chair. There was one window which overlooked the farm, but no curtains. The hut seemed pretty shaky, as if it might fall down and collapse at any moment.

"This is where you'll sleep," said Dovid's new boss. He sounded very reasonable as he explained the arrangements. "All the other workers will be living in a cabin together. They are much older than you, and that may bother you. You'll be a lot better off in your own place."

Old man Boris went on. "Listen, I expect hard work from you. I don't hire people because they're nice. I hire people who can work. If you can't keep up with the others, you won't have this job for very long.

"I expect you to pick fifty potatoes an hour. We work about twelve hours a day, so that's six hundred potatoes. I understand that the first day you have to get used to the work, so you might not pick that many. But after that I won't accept any excuses."

Dovid would not work alongside the other men, Boris continued. He would work alone in this particular field. This, too, was for his own good. Dovid could see the men in the distance — they were quite far away.

Dovid quickly agreed to everything. He started picking potatoes at once and found it back-breaking work. His shoulders hurt terribly, and he had an awful ache in his back. Soon his fingers were raw and bleeding.

After an hour, Dovid counted the potatoes in his basket and found he'd picked only twelve. He decided to ignore the pain and work harder. The second hour he picked eighteen. Most of the day he averaged about twenty potatoes an hour. Finally, at nightfall, when he could no longer see, old man Boris came and told him it was time to stop. The farmer counted Dovid's potatoes, shook his head in disgust, and told the boy he'd have to do far better the following day. Now he could return to his cabin and eat his supper.

Dovid didn't believe Boris's story about the other men being a threat to him. He didn't like being forced to eat alone in his little hut. But he knew he was lucky to have a job at all, and if he spoke up, he'd be fired. So he didn't say a word.

Dovid was starving when he reached the hut. The supper was meager — a piece of black bread, hard and stale, at least three days old. With it was some soup, mostly broth with something dark floating in it. It could have been a piece of meat. It looked more like a piece of skin. At least, he thought with a sigh, it gave a bit of taste to the soup. There was also a small plate of cold boiled potatoes.

Though the meal was unappealing, Dovid wolfed down the food, famished after the long day's work. He had to eat to survive. It didn't matter if he liked it. Nor did it matter if the food was kosher. Dovid had long stopped caring about that.

After supper, Dovid lay down on his narrow cot and collapsed. His hands and nails were bleeding. His back was incredibly sore, and he doubted he could ever stand up straight again. Every muscle ached. As soon as his head hit the pillow, he was asleep.

After what seemed only a few minutes, Dovid felt a rough hand shaking him awake. It was old man Boris himself. "Get up, you lazy Jew! Move it!"

Dovid looked out the window, expecting to see the pitch black of night, but it was morning. Dovid had never felt so sick and exhausted. But he had no choice. He had to get up.

"Hurry!" said old man Boris, dragging Dovid out of bed. As soon as he reassured himself that Dovid wouldn't fall asleep again, the mean old man left, slamming the door behind him.

Dovid got up, washed, and sat at the table where his breakfast waited. There was some hot tea. At least, he thought it was tea. It was dark and sweet and felt good going down. There was also a large slice of black bread. It wouldn't be enough to give him the strength he needed, but he ate it quickly and was grateful for it.

As soon as Dovid started walking to the fields, old man Boris directed him once again to a field far away from the other men. Dovid had hoped to talk to Peter and perhaps meet some of the others. But that was not to be.

Every hour Dovid counted the number of potatoes in his basket. Often there were thirty or thirty-five. He was working like a slave. How could anyone possibly pick fifty?

Dovid's lunch, bread with cheese and some water, was brought to him in the field by the hired man who'd talked to Peter on the road. He ate it in a few minutes, and then went right back to work.

Until the very last light of day, Dovid worked alone in the field. Then old man Boris came for him and took him back to his hut for his supper, which was similar to the one he'd had the previous night. Again he collapsed into bed like a dead man, and again he was awakened by the rough hand and raging voice of old man Boris.

BETRAYAL

Unknown to Dovid, Peter and the other men were having a much better time of it. They were served a large, hearty breakfast each morning. Old man Boris didn't want to waste money, but he also wanted the most work he could get from his workers. Lunches were substantial, and supper was plentiful, too. It included soup, meat, potatoes, and beer, and they could eat as much of everything as they wanted.

When the men reached their cabin each evening, they talked for hours. There was a lot of cameraderie among them, for many knew each other from coming year after year to work for old man Boris. They played cards and passed the time pleasantly until bedtime. They had no idea of how Dovid was suffering.

An entire week passed, and Dovid was getting weaker and weaker. Although he pushed himself to the limit of his strength, he could never pick more than thirty-five potatoes an hour. Every day old man Boris yelled, "If you can't pick more than that, then I can't keep you. I'm not in the habit of giving charity."

Dovid had no idea that the other men were picking only twenty-five potatoes an hour at the most. They were not working nearly as hard as he was. Dovid didn't realize that he was being tricked. He didn't know why he was working in a different field, and old man Boris didn't want him to find out.

Finally Sunday morning came — payday. The workers boasted about what they'd soon do in the city, about what they would drink and what they would eat. Most of them would come back to the farm as poor as they'd been before getting their money.

Dovid waited eagerly for his pay. He knew old man Boris was cheap, but at ten rubles a day it was still a lot more money than he'd seen in a long time. He was hoping for sixty rubles like all the other men. When each man's name was called, he was handed an envelope with his cash inside. The men began filling up the carriage that would take them to town. They were in a very cheerful mood, laughing and joking around.

Finally, only Dovid was left. He walked up to old man Boris and said respectfully, "Excuse me, sir, but have you forgotten me? Where is my pay?"

Boris looked at Dovid disdainfully and exclaimed, "You expect me to pay you? Don't you realize how much it costs to feed you each day? Don't you realize that you have your own hut? None of the other men have that privilege. And you're picking only thirty-five potatoes an hour. You're not even doing the work of one man!

"I charge three rubles a day for the hut and seven rubles a day for the food. The way you've been working, you only deserve six rubles a day. That means you owe me four rubles for each of the six days you've been here. That's twenty-four rubles. If you don't start working faster, I'm not even going to give you the chance to earn that money. Now get back to your hut and rest up for tomorrow! You've got work to do."

Dovid couldn't believe it. He'd worked like a slave, and now he was being told he owed the old man money! How could he owe Boris money when he was working more than twelve hours a day doing back-breaking work? How could he owe him money when he was barely being fed at all?

Dovid didn't know what to do. All he could think of was that he still had a warm bed to sleep in every night. He still had some food to put in his mouth and something to fill his time. He made up his mind to try one more week. He would see if he could pick more potatoes in order to earn his wages. Then, he hoped, even if he had to repay old man Boris, he would still have thirty-six rubles left for himself.

Dovid rested all of Sunday. By now his back had gotten used to the work, and his fingers had developed calluses that made it easier for him to dig out the potatoes without cutting himself. He had great hopes of picking his quota of potatoes the next day.

The next morning, before the break of dawn, old man

Boris shook him awake as usual. "Get up, you lazy, good-for-nothing Jew!" he yelled in Dovid's ear. "It's time for work! This week you'd better work like a real man, not like a one-handed Jewish beggar!"

Dovid jumped out of bed, gobbled his breakfast, and was off to the field. He worked so hard and so fast that he was picking forty-three potatoes an hour, a tremendous improvement from the week before. Dovid was very proud of his output, and he was sure old man Boris would be pleased with him this time.

At the end of the day, Dovid was proud. Old man Boris counted his potatoes and said, "Well, for your second week, forty-three potatoes an hour isn't bad, but it's not enough. You'll still owe me money at the end of the week. Can't we get some real work out of you?"

That night Dovid again had his bread and watery soup. Then, as always, he fell into a deep sleep.

The next morning he was at it again. He worked like a demon, and every hour he counted his potatoes. As he watched the pile grow, he was pleased to see he was up to forty-eight an hour. That evening, when old man Boris counted the potatoes, there was a faint smile on his face. "You're almost working like a good Russian boy," he said with a hint of warmth. "I'm really proud of you. Keep it up and you'll really do well. In fact, I have a special treat for you after dinner tonight."

What was the treat? Half a rotten apple that Dovid could barely force down!

That whole week, Dovid worked harder than he'd ever worked before. On some days, he was able to pick fifty an hour. For the most part, though, he picked an average of forty-seven potatoes an hour. Still, he felt as though he deserved to get paid this time. But deserving the money and getting it were two different things.

On Sunday, there was a repeat of the previous week's scene. The men lined up for their pay envelopes, and each one's name was called. And again, there was no mention of Dovid.

"Sir," he said to old man Boris, "this week I know I've earned a paycheck." Dovid looked his boss directly in the eye. He was determined to get what he deserved.

The pale blue eyes were filled with scorn. "Yes, my dear young man. Things are going a lot better. But the way I've calculated it, this week, instead of owing me twenty-four rubles, you owe me only eight. That's a nice improvement, but now you owe me a total of thirty-two rubles. Maybe next week you can make it up."

Dovid realized he was in an impossible situation. You don't work your heart out for somebody and then owe him money at the end of the week. He began to realize what had happened. As soon as old man Boris heard that he had no parents or friends to look out for him, his watery blue eyes had lit up. He knew at once that he could make money at the expense of a poor orphan. Then and there he made up his mind that he would no longer work for old man Boris.

Dovid knew he had to leave, but he also knew that if he

asked Boris's permission, the first thing his taskmaster would do would be to demand the thirty-two rubles he claimed Dovid owed him. Dovid had no money to pay him, and he feared that Boris would send for the police to arrest him. He had only one choice: to sneak off without old man Boris finding out.

That night, instead of going to sleep right after supper, Dovid gathered his few possessions and made for the door. It was locked! He was always so tired after slaving away all day that every night he'd collapsed on his cot right after supper. He'd never tried to go out. Now he realized he was being held prisoner. How could he possibly escape?

Dovid checked the window — it had bars on it. There was no way he could climb through it. Now he was truly afraid.

He sat down on his bed and thought about what he could do. Boris had a dog named Ripper which was always tied up during the day, but at night it ran loose. Ripper was a German shepherd. The dog was huge and had sharp teeth, but it was painfully thin. Obviously Ripper didn't get much to eat either.

When the dog was out with his master, he was always snarling at the men. Given the opportunity, he'd be glad to sink his teeth into any one of them. Dovid knew that if he'd try to leave, Ripper would attack him and tear him apart.

The next day at work, Dovid thought long and hard about how to make his escape. After a full day of picking potatoes, a plan began to take shape in his mind.

Betrayal

That night he told Boris that there were rats in the hut and that they were disturbing his sleep. Dovid knew he wouldn't care except for the fact that if Dovid didn't sleep well, he couldn't do his work.

Old man Boris gave him a bag of rat poison, just as Dovid had hoped. The poison would be his weapon against Ripper.

For the next three nights, as hungry as he was, Dovid saved the small piece of meat from his soup. On the third night, he tied the pieces together with a bit of string, leaving a little hole in the middle. In the hole he put the rat poison, packing the meat around it in such a way that the poison would not be detected. He would throw the meat to Ripper. The poison would keep the dog from attacking Dovid.

Dovid wasn't sure his plan would work, but he had to try. He certainly wasn't going to stay on this farm week after week and go further into debt.

His next problem was how to get the door open, but he had an idea for that as well. The next day in the field, he waited until old man Boris left him for a minute. He screamed across the next field loud enough for Peter to hear. "Peter! I haven't had a chance to talk to you for a long time! How are you?"

Peter screamed back to him, "Not bad. The work's easy enough. We only have a few more weeks, so you'd better save your money. We're going back to begging again. See you soon, Dimitri!"

But Dovid wasn't finished. He yelled, "Peter, I need a little favor from you. Can you help me out?"

Peter shouted back, "Of course, my friend. What do you need?"

Dovid shouted, "Peter, every night Boris locks my door. He does it to protect me from the other workers. But sometimes at night I need fresh air. Tonight, at around eleven o'clock, would you come and open the door for me? Old man Boris will never know."

Peter yelled, "I don't have a problem with that."

"But there's just one thing," Dovid added. "You'll have to get around the old man's guard dog. Maybe you can bring a cat in a bag and let it out when you come near. That would take Ripper's attention off of you!"

"I'll figure something out, Dimitri. Don't worry!"

Dovid shouted back a "thank you" just as old man Boris appeared in the distance. Dovid prayed that his plan would work. It was the first time he had prayed since leaving his hometown.

That night, when old man Boris finally sent Dovid back to his hut, the boy did not go to sleep. He ate slowly, and then lay down to rest, waiting for Peter to arrive.

The meat with the rat poison was ready. So was a small container of water for his much-anticipated journey. He knew that if he did escape he would need water in order to survive. Every now and then he looked out of the window for signs of Ripper. He hoped that by the time he was ready to escape Ripper would be in another part of the field.

At eleven o'clock, Dovid prayed again. This time he

prayed that Peter had done what he had agreed to do. Still, at the last moment Dovid decided that eleven o'clock was too early. Perhaps there would still be people up and about. Even at midnight he felt he would be taking a chance to step outside.

Dovid made up his mind not to budge until one o'clock in the morning. He sat on his bed, half asleep, trying to save his energy. Finally, it was time for him to go. He tried the door, testing it to see if it would open without any noise. Exactly as he had hoped, the door slid open. His eyes took in the area outside his hut, and, as far as he could see, there was no sign of Ripper.

What Dovid did not realize was that just to the right of the hut Boris sat, waiting in a chair. In his grubby hand was a huge leather whip.

Obviously Peter was not as good a friend as Dovid had thought. Peter loved money, and old man Boris had a lot of it. As soon as Peter heard Dovid's story, he'd suspected the truth. He had never understood why Dovid was alone in that hut and why he had always picked his potatoes in a different field.

When Dimitri asked him to unlock the door, Peter realized that the boy was being locked in on purpose. Boris would not lock the door without a reason. He realized that Dovid had some kind of plan which old man Boris would love to hear about.

That evening, as soon as work was over, he strolled over to old man Boris and called him aside. "Sir," he confided with a sly smile, "I have some very valuable information to share with you. Something I'm sure you'd love to know."

Old man Boris eyed him suspiciously. "What could you know that I'd want to know? Tell me now and get it over with."

But Peter was a sly fellow. He realized that information was worth money. "Sure," he replied, "I'll let you know what it is. But you'll have to pay me if you want me to talk. After all, don't I deserve a reward for giving you important information?"

Boris hemmed and hawed and finally agreed to give Peter fifty rubles. Of course, the condition was that if old man Boris was not satisfied with the information, Peter would get nothing.

Peter smiled and said, "Don't worry, this is certainly worth fifty rubles to you. At *least* fifty rubles!" Then he told Boris exactly what the boy had told him. "He's expecting me to unlock the door at eleven o'clock," Peter concluded.

Old man Boris shook Peter's hand, gave him the money, and said, "All right, it's a fair deal. Here's the money. Now listen, Peter, unlock the door as Dimitri asked."

Peter couldn't understand why, after paying him fifty rubles, old man Boris would let the boy escape. But he certainly wasn't going to ask any questions. If this was what Boris wanted, he was more than happy to oblige. What he didn't know was that old man Boris planned to catch Dovid escaping and beat the boy within an inch of his life. Then all the workers and all the townspeople would realize that nobody should dare to cross old man Boris. He would put out the word that Dovid was a robber, that he had stolen thirty-two rubles from him and was trying to escape without paying what he owed. That way, everyone would know that old man Boris didn't wait for the police; he took care of things himself and handed out a much harsher punishment. The wicked old man relished the thought of beating up the boy.

So now Boris sat, waiting impatiently. But he'd woken up before five o'clock that morning and could barely keep his eyes open. By midnight he fell into a deep sleep. He didn't even notice the door to Dovid's cabin slowly opening at one o'clock in the morning.

ESCAPE

As soon as Dovid thought he was safe, he started running. It was three hundred yards to the edge of the farm. There he would climb the fence. On the other side was the forest. After climbing the fence he'd be safe from Ripper. And if he could make it through the forest without getting caught, there would be no stopping him.

Dovid was almost at the fence. Only another fifty yards and he'd be there.

All of a sudden, there was a snarl behind him. Ripper! He turned and faced the dog straight on. The animal's eyes bulged in the moonlight. Ripper was foaming at the mouth. He bared his fangs and was about to attack!

Dovid had to save himself. Quickly he wrapped his jacket around his arm in an attempt to shield his body. He raised his arm and slowly began backing toward the fence. Dovid was only ten yards away, but Ripper was getting ready to lunge. It was time for Dovid to throw the poisoned meat.

Dovid prayed to the Almighty and aimed. Ripper got excited when he saw the meat. Instead of leaping toward Dovid, he lunged for the meat and swallowed it in one gulp.

Dovid expected the dog to drop dead then and there, but nothing happened. Ripper turned to Dovid once again. In a frenzy, he jumped for Dovid's throat. Dovid raised his arm for protection, and Ripper's piercing fangs dug deep into Dovid's arm. Though the jacket took most of the attack, an eight-inch slash ripped Dovid's flesh, and blood gushed as if from a fountain.

Dovid was in shock, but he knew he had only a moment before Ripper attacked again. Once more, he raised his arm to defend himself. Ripper struck again. This time Dovid was able to shove Ripper's snout away before the monstrous dog caused any more damage. Ripper retreated, then circled, preparing for a third attack.

Dovid began to feel weak. He was losing blood, and his hard work and poor diet had taken their toll. Ripper leaped once more for Dovid's throat, but this time a miracle saved him. Halfway through his lunge Ripper's body went into spasms, and he collapsed. The rat poison had finally taken effect. Dovid took a second to catch his breath, then rushed toward the fence, blood pouring from his wound.

But Dovid was still in terrible danger. Ripper's barking and snarling had awakened Boris, sitting near the hut. Immediately he discovered that Dovid had taken off. An evil smile lit up the face of Dovid's taskmaster. He had trained Ripper well! Boris took off in pursuit, his black leather whip at the ready.

Dovid was at the fence. As he was climbing over it, Boris reached the body of his dog. He cursed in anger, then noticed the blood on the grass. Boris followed the trail of blood to the fence. Sure enough he found Dovid frantically trying to scramble over the fence in his haste to get away. Boris brought his whip down hard on Dovid's leg a moment before his feet landed on the other side. The whip slashed Dovid's ankle, and his screams reverberated through the forest. But, in spite of everything, Dovid was on the other side of the fence. He had no time to think about his pain. He ran as fast as he could!

Old man Boris knew that the pitch-dark forest was a perfect place to hide. It would be impossible for him to catch Dovid without help.

Boris raced toward the cabin of the sleeping men. He banged on the doors, and everyone jumped up, wondering what crazy old Boris wanted in the middle of the night.

Boris screamed, "Quick, men, get moving! That boy, Dimitri, he stole my money. He's trying to escape. Help me catch him. Get up now!"

The men looked at their nasty old boss without pity. None of them made any effort to get out of bed.

"Please, Boris, let us go back to sleep," said Oleg, yawning and stretching his arms.

"We have a long day ahead of us tomorrow," said Vladimir. "We need our rest."

"Let the boy go," said Alex. "A boy his age can't do much work anyway. He's not worth running after."

But Boris was now completely out of control. His hatred of Jews made him forget his dislike of giving away money. It made him forget everything but his desire to get Dovid back in his clutches. He screamed at his men, "I'll give you the day off tomorrow if you help me now for three hours. And I'll give you triple pay. I'm going to find that thief! No one can steal from me and get away with it! No one!"

The wicked old man had to stop and catch his breath. His next words really got the men's attention. "Whoever finds Dimitri will be rewarded a hundred rubles. This I promise you!"

The men wasted no more time. They jumped out of bed and got moving. Triple pay for only three hours and the next day off! Boris's offer of a hundred rubles to the man who found Dimitri ensured that everyone would do his best to catch the scoundrel. While the men threw on their clothes, Boris had one last thing to say. His announcement so shocked the men that they gasped in astonishment, and the room fell silent.

"I don't care," said Boris, "whether you bring back the boy dead or alive. You'll still get your hundred rubles!"

At first the men were horrified, but then they began to turn it over in their minds. *It's a lot easier to bring home a dead body than a struggling boy,* they rationalized. *Why should we go through the trouble of bringing him back alive? Better to kill him and bring the body back.*

Many of the workers had been brought up in fairly decent homes, but they had long forgotten their parents' teachings in their lust for money. To them life was cheap, and they would let nothing stand in the way of a hundred-ruble reward.

Boris handed every man a torch. He pointed them in Dovid's direction, and over twenty men set out to hunt the boy as they would an animal. Each was hoping to be the lucky one, the one who would bring Dovid's body back to the farm.

But that was not all the old man had in mind. Although Ripper had been his guard dog and his means of keeping his workers in line, Boris also had three hunting dogs, each trained to hunt down its prey by scent.

Old man Boris yelled for the dog trainer. The man brought the animals with him into the small hut where Dovid had lived for the past three weeks. The dogs sniffed at his bed and belongings. The trainer could scarcely hold them back as they charged forward, determined to track down the owner of the scent.

Despite his age, old man Boris was hot on the trainer's heels. His anger fueled him on.

Dovid hadn't been able to get far in the short time it had taken Boris to organize the search. Dovid's injuries were slowing him down. And, as he raced through the bushes, sharp branches did their terrible work on his face, arms, and legs, covering him with scratches and welts.

After awhile Dovid heard distant shouts, and he knew they were pursuing him. When he heard the yelping of the hunting dogs he feared for his life as never before. Just at that moment, his feet plunged into something wet, and he realized he was running through a small stream. He had heard once that a person's scent can be masked by water. Perhaps he could outwit the dogs.

Dovid waded into the small stream, making his way over slippery rocks. Then he climbed onto land and began to run as fast as he could.

After fifteen minutes of running he collapsed. The loss of blood, the fear, the pain, the exhaustion — it all finally caught up with him. With his last remaining strength, he dragged himself from the forest path. As best he could, he pulled a few handfuls of leaves over his body in an effort to hide himself.

The men were getting closer, and he could hear them screaming, "I know he's here! We'll catch him! Don't forget — it's dead or alive."

Dovid knew how vulnerable he was. Men kept passing within five or six inches of where he lay, but Dovid lay undiscovered under the leaves.

When the dogs reached the stream, they began to cross. But in midstream they suddenly stopped, confused. Angry because they'd been thrown off the scent, the animals began to bark and yelp, running around in circles in the water. Dovid's trick had worked.

Old man Boris was enraged. He cursed the dog trainer and sent him back to the farm. "This is not the last you'll hear about this! You call yourself a dog trainer? You are a nothing! A nobody!" The dog trainer didn't even attempt to answer.

He walked slowly back to the farm, wondering what punishment was in store for him.

Meanwhile, undaunted by the failure of the dogs to pick up Dovid's scent, Boris pressed on. He kept after his men, bullying and hounding them mercilessly to continue the search. But when the three hours were up, Dovid still had not been found.

The men started to complain. "Sir," said Vasily, the lead hand, "you said three hours, and three hours are up. We have to go back to sleep. We worked hard yesterday and can't continue like this."

Boris was bitter, but he knew he'd better give in, or he'd lose what little respect the workers had for him. "Okay," he replied. "A bargain is a bargain. You can all go back now."

How Boris hated himself for setting a three-hour time limit! He had been certain he'd find Dimitri right away. Boris seldom made these kinds of mistakes — that was why he was so rich. He could kick himself for letting the boy get away from him so easily!

The men returned to the cabin, leaving the old man alone in the forest. Boris realized it would be impossible to find Dimitri before sunrise. The boy had actually managed to escape.

Reluctantly, Boris went home to get some sleep. But he was already making new plans. He would organize an even larger search party in the morning. He would go to the police bright and early and tell the chief that Dimitri was a robber who had stolen vast sums of money from him. The old miser was sure the police chief would send officers to search for the boy. After all, he, Boris, was the largest landholder in the village. No one, he reasoned, would doubt the truth of his story.

At the crack of dawn, Dovid woke up. His arm was swollen and caked with blood and dirt. Mud had entered the wound, and Dovid felt the heat of an infection setting in. His exhaustion knew no bounds. He knew, however, that there was no way he could stay where he was.

With great difficulty, Dovid dragged himself on his hands and knees back to the stream. He cried in pain as he rolled his body into the water. He let the water run over his wounds to clean them and prevent the spread of the infection.

Lying in the icy water was agony. Dovid's face, arms, and legs stung from the cuts. His ankle also began to swell, and he knew he was in urgent need of a doctor. But he forced himself to lie there, knowing the cold water would help his ankle and clean his wounds.

Dovid drank deeply from the stream. His thirst was unquenchable. He made sure, however, to keep his head above the water, for he was so weak he could be pulled down by the current. Afterward, he pulled himself out of the stream. He took off his shirt and tore it in half. With one half he bandaged his arm. With the other half he bound his throbbing ankle. Then, slowly, he started walking away from the stream, knowing that if he didn't get far away, it would be only a matter of time before his wicked boss found him.

Dovid walked for almost an hour, each step more painful than the last. His clothes were wet, and his arm was still oozing blood. Eventually, he collapsed again and fell into a deep sleep. He slept the whole day and right through the following night.

THE GOOD SOLDIER

When Dovid awoke the next morning, he could barely move. When he looked down at his arm, he shuddered at the sight of it. The infection had made its way up to the shoulder.

Dovid gathered his strength and lifted his head to take a look around. In the thick of the forest, right near where Dovid had collapsed, he saw three soldiers. The young men were bent over a pit and were pulling a crate out of it. When they opened the crate, they began unloading rifles into a canvas bag. One of the soldiers went to sit under a tree, for the sun was hot, even that early in the morning. As soon as he sat down, he noticed Dovid.

The soldier yelled to his friends, "Hey, there's a dead child here! A young boy! Come quick!"

The others rushed to their friend's side. Sure enough, there lay the body of a young boy, perhaps fourteen years old, right by the edge of the road. As they stared down at

Dovid, wondering what to do, the first soldier said, "Wait, his chest is moving! He's still breathing!"

The soldier, whose name was Sergei, bent down beside Dovid and heard his heartbeat. He shouted to his friends, "We've got to save him! We'll take him back to our base, and the doctor will take care of him. Quick, there's not a minute to lose!"

The other two soldiers looked at Sergei in surprise. "Listen," said one, "we've got to carry these guns all the way back. It's a good hour's walk from here to the base. We can't carry this boy as well."

"Just leave him. He's almost dead anyway," said the other.

Sergei could not believe what his friends were saying. "We're talking about a boy's life. We can't just leave him here. It's unthinkable!"

The other two just stood there, saying nothing.

Without another word to his companions, Sergei gently put Dovid over his shoulder and carried him all the way to the base. It took him much longer than an hour, since he had to stop often to rest. Although Dovid did not weigh a lot, he was still a heavy burden for one man to carry so far. But for Sergei there was no choice. He felt a responsibility to save this boy's life. He had a brother back home who was about the same age as Dovid. Wouldn't he want a stranger to help him if the boy were ever in such a situation?

Finally, Sergei reached the base. It was a secret base, hidden from all but the commanders and the few soldiers stationed there. Sergei was among a group of rebel soldiers fighting against the Russian army. They had been losing to the government troops and were now in hiding, readying themselves for another attack.

The base had a doctor and a well-stocked infirmary. Sergei brought Dovid straight to the infirmary and lay him on the nearest bed. Then he went off in search of the doctor.

"Doctor, come quick!" exclaimed Sergei when he found him. "There's a young boy who looks like he could die at any moment!"

The doctor was surprised. "Who is this boy?" he asked in amazement. "There are no boys in our army!"

Sergei explained how he'd found Dovid and how he'd carried him back with him so the boy could get medical attention.

"Listen," said the doctor, "I work hard, and when there is a fight on, I sometimes have to work for more than twenty-four hours at a stretch. Now that things are a little easy, let me relax. It's not my job to look after boys. Find another doctor."

Sergei's fury knew no limits. He'd seen the true character of his soldier friends. Now a doctor was refusing to save a life!

Sergei screamed in anger, "Doctor, I insist you look after this boy! I brought him here with great trouble and at tremendous personal sacrifice. You must at least try to help him. I insist!"

The doctor saw Sergei would not give up. Sighing, he

lifted himself off the couch and went with Sergei to the infirmary.

It didn't take the doctor long to assess Dovid's condition. He told Sergei that the boy was suffering from blood poisoning. He had an advanced case of pneumonia, and there was little likelihood he would pull through.

But Sergei was persistent. "Doctor," Sergei pleaded, "this boy means a lot to me. Can't you try? I swear to you, I'll take care of him. I won't leave his bedside until he's healed. Give him a chance!"

Reluctantly, the doctor gave in. "All right, you win. But I want you to understand one thing: I stop work at five. I don't come back until eight o'clock the next morning. Don't call me for anything on my off hours. If you want to look after him, that's fine with me. There's a chance he can be saved. I'll do what I can during the hours I'm available."

So the deal was struck. The doctor immediately went to work on Dovid. He gave him the medicines he needed and tended to his arm and ankle. He cleaned out Dovid's wounds and stitched them up as best he could. In spite of himself, the doctor's heart began to soften as he looked after the boy. He was just a child, after all.

For three days Dovid lay unconscious. He couldn't eat or drink on his own, but every hour or so Sergei poured a bit of water into his parched mouth. Whatever Dovid seemed to need, Sergei provided. Slowly, as the doctor took an increasing interest, changing Dovid's dressings and giving him the proper medicines, a small improvement could be seen.

After three days it became apparent that a real miracle had taken place. Dovid was on his way to recovery. The doctor had not told Sergei he had considered amputating Dovid's arm at the shoulder because of the blood poisoning. Now the infection was beginning to heal, and it seemed Dovid would not lose his arm after all.

Each day Dovid became stronger. Soon he was sitting up in bed, drinking soup and eating pudding. The doctor called it a miracle. Eventually, Dovid was walking again. His arm was still sore, and he was thin, but he was slowly getting his appetite back.

All this time Sergei had never asked Dovid where he came from or how he came to be lying on the grass near the side of the road. If anyone deserved an answer it was Sergei. Yet he controlled himself because he knew that in time the boy would surely offer him an explanation.

But Dovid remembered that from the moment old man Boris found out how alone he really was, he took advantage of him and treated him differently from anybody else. He was frightened that if he told Sergei the truth the same thing would happen.

It took many days, during which Sergei cared for Dovid devotedly, for Dovid to begin trusting the soldier. In time, Dovid told him most of the details of how he had ended up at the roadside. He told Sergei about old man Boris and how he'd been accused of being a robber. Dovid also mentioned that the police might be looking for him. He swore to Sergei that he had stolen nothing. How could he have worked week after week for the evil old man and still owe him money?

Sergei told Dovid not to worry — this was a rebel base, and the police didn't even know it existed. Dovid was safe as long as he was on the army base with Sergei.

"How long can I stay?" Dovid asked. "I'm not part of the rebel army."

"Don't worry, Dimitri," Sergei reassured him. "I've spoken to Captain Mikalovitch. Since there's no one else to look after you, he's agreed to let you to stay on the base on the condition that you cause us no trouble. You can sleep in my tent."

Dovid accepted Sergei's offer with tears of relief. He was more than happy to stay at the army base.

Sergei made sure that Dovid had enough to eat and that nobody bothered him. Dovid had three good meals a day and warm clothing instead of his old rags. He came to know most of the soldiers by name and even became friendly with some of them. Some regarded him as a pest, but most thought he was a friendly, likable kid. Dovid had grown to like the men in his tent. He was happy to be among them, and since he caused no one any trouble, he was allowed to stay.

Dovid kept asking Sergei, "Is there any way I can help you? Everyone seems to have a job to do. Maybe I can do something, too."

Sergei realized that Dovid needed something to occupy his time. "One of my jobs is to help out in the kitchen, peeling potatoes. Would you like to do that?"

Dovid jumped at the chance. "Sure, Sergei. I'd be happy to do it."

That afternoon Dovid spent several hours helping out in the kitchen. It was boring work, but it made Dovid feel useful. That job was only the beginning. Every day from then on Dovid helped Sergei with his chores.

Sergei had a friend named Igor who lived in the same tent. After Dovid started taking over Sergei's jobs, Igor thought maybe he could get the same service. One day he sauntered over to Sergei and said, "Listen, Sergei, that boy has nothing much to do. Why not let Dimitri help me, too?"

Sergei replied, "It's up to Dimitri. If he doesn't care, I don't either."

From then on, Dovid did not only Sergei's work but Igor's work as well. Igor began to appreciate Dovid, but Sergei remained his closest companion.

Dovid also like to watch as Sergei cleaned his gun and practiced shooting. Noticing Dovid's curiosity, Sergei decided to teach Dovid how to use a gun. He explained to him how to open a gun to clean it and how to keep it well oiled. Dovid began practicing shooting at the target range, and after a while he was joining the men at shooting practice.

Dovid also learned how to throw a knife and was becoming proficient in hand-to-hand combat. As he grew taller, he began to wear the army uniform and appeared to be as much of a soldier as any of the others.

NIGHT WATCH

For months the rebel group had hidden in their hideout, preparing to attack the Russian army. They feared being discovered, so they kept a constant lookout. Guards patrolled the camp in three-hour shifts throughout the night.

One afternoon, Igor came back from lunch and noticed that his name was posted for guard duty between midnight and three in the morning. Igor hated this job most of all. He hated waking up in the middle of the night and standing in the dark, staring at nothing and listening for sounds that never came. He found it boring, and the only thing that kept him awake was the knowledge that falling asleep during guard duty was punishable by death.

That afternoon he sought out Dimitri. "My friend," said Igor, "you don't seem to mind taking over some of our jobs."

"Sure, Igor," replied Dovid. "I don't mind at all. I want to earn my keep."

Igor replied, "Well I've got something really special for you tonight."

"What is it, Igor?"

Igor explained, "I don't know if you've ever done this before, but it's a simple job. You take a gun and you stand at one of the guardposts for three hours. Then you can go back to sleep. Of course, if we were attacked, which is highly unlikely, you'd have to shoot your gun to alert the rest us. I wouldn't worry about that, though. It hasn't happened yet, so why should it happen the very night you become a guard?"

Dovid wasn't sure how to respond. He was very excited about being offered such an important job. He also thought staying up late at night might be fun. But he was sure it was against the rules. The commander wouldn't allow a fifteen-year-old boy to guard the entire camp. He was mature and responsible, and he knew how to use a gun. But he was still only fifteen.

Who would find out? Probably no one, but still... Dovid decided to ask Sergei what to do. That afternoon, after Sergei's target practice, Dovid pulled him aside and told him what Igor had asked him to do.

Sergei grunted. "It's not a good idea. I would never ask you to do guard duty for me. I'm not sure if you'd get into trouble, but Igor would. He's not allowed to give this duty to anybody else without notifying the captain. Certainly not to a civilian. My advice is not to do it, but it's more his problem than yours if you get caught."

Dovid went back to Igor. Politely and graciously he explained that he could not accept the job. The soldier wasn't happy, but there was nothing he could do. From then on, though, Igor started pestering Dovid to take over his guard duty.

Dovid knew that in order to stay in the camp he had to remain friendly with everyone in his tent. He could see how important this was to Igor, so finally he gave in and agreed to guard.

At midnight Igor woke him up, handed him his gun, and wished him good luck. Dovid was very excited. A few times he heard sounds that troubled him, but after listening carefully he decided that it was just some forest animals making noise in the distance. Once he heard a tree branch cracking, but then he heard the fluttering of a bird as it flew away. Guarding was such a simple task. Why had Igor made such a big deal about it?

The next morning, when Igor thanked him, Dovid said, "Listen, Igor, I don't mind doing this at all. It was actually fun. Let me know the next time you want me, and I'll do it for you again."

Igor was thrilled. "Well, guard duty comes up every three or four days. I'll be sure to let you know."

That day Sergei came over to Dovid, looking furious. He had found out about the guard duty. "Dimitri," he said, "I've looked after you in the past, and I'll continue to do so. But this is not a wise idea. Peeling potatoes is one thing; being on guard duty is another. It's a soldier's responsibility."

Dovid liked Sergei and didn't want to lose his friendship, but he didn't see anything wrong with it. So he stayed silent, and, as he intended, Sergei took that as an agreement not to do it again.

Several nights later, it was Igor's turn to guard again, and once more Dovid agreed to take over for him. This time, though, it was not to be such a simple job. After months of tracking and receiving different bits of information, the Russian army had finally located the rebel hideout. A nighttime attack, they reasoned, would give them the best likelihood of wiping out the rebels. The element of surprise would work in their favor.

Just after midnight, specially trained soldiers were sent to locate the night guards. The men guarding the rebel camp could not be shot, for the sound of gunfire would awaken the others. The guards could be killed only by hand or by knife.

The government soldiers knew there were three men standing guard at the three possible approaches to the camp. One guard was smoking a cigarette; this made him easy to spot in the dark. Two scouts slipped silently through the forest and pierced the guard's heart before he had the chance to call out. The second guard was half asleep, waiting for his guard duty to end. His silhouette was highlighted against the light of the moon. In one split second a knife whizzed through the night air, and the guard breathed his last breath. Now Dovid was the only guard left alive. He alone would have to save the army base.

Dovid stood at full alert when he heard a rustle in the

bushes. Frowning, he turned his head toward the sound. Again the bushes rustled. Was it a wild animal or an enemy soldier? Dovid lifted his rifle to his shoulder and aimed in the direction of the sound. After staring intently at the same spot for more than ten minutes, he was positive he saw movement.

Dovid cocked his rifle and waited. If the shape moved, he would shoot first and ask questions later. Every fiber of his body told him it was an emergency, and he wasn't mistaken. Someone was hiding in the bushes with a knife in his hand!

Dovid shot and screamed for help. Dozens of soldiers charged toward him, toward the army camp. But his warning shot had done its job — everyone in the camp had been alerted. They quickly readied themselves to repel the attack, and in mere seconds Dovid's comrades had guns in their hands.

The battle raged throughout the night, and both sides suffered heavy casualties. Dovid, who ran back into the camp after firing the warning shot, saw three of the men who lived in his tent fall to enemy fire. Two died immediately and one lay on the ground, moaning for hours. No one could help him, because he was right in the line of enemy fire.

Somehow, by morning the rebel soldiers had succeeded in stemming the enemy attack. A retreat was called, and the attackers vanished as quickly as they'd come.

Captain Mikalovitch was badly wounded, but was still firmly in charge. Despite his pain, his voice was strong: "Quick, every able-bodied man account for all the others! Find the wounded! Bring the dead into the center of the camp! Who will volunteer to help the doctor? Bring warm blankets. Now! We need food! We need hot water. Quick! There's not a moment to lose!"

Dovid forced himself to move. He brought hot water to the wounded, listening to their tragic cries of pain and suffering. As he worked, Dovid prayed that Sergei and Igor were still alive. He could not bear to think what life would be like without Sergei.

As he moved along the rows of wounded, he spotted his best friend in a corner. Dovid sighed with relief. Sergei was helping somebody, as always. Dovid ran over to Sergei and hugged him in sheer joy. "Sergei!" he cried, tears running down his face.

Sergei, too, wept openly. "Dimitri, you're alive!"

By noon the situation was under control. The captain's wounds were dressed, and he felt strong enough to continue his command. Most of the tents were either burned or knocked down. Many men lay on the ground, out in the open, totally worn out. They had been fighting fiercely since the middle of the night and had spent the entire morning helping the wounded and burying the dead.

Captain Mikalovitch went back to his tent, but he could not rest. He had to find out what had happened. It was important to know how to prevent a similar tragedy. He looked at his roster sheet to see who had been on guard duty that night and saw Igor's name there. He sent his men to find out whether any of the guards had survived. He was told that two of them had been found dead at their posts, but Igor was still alive. Captain Mikalovitch was grateful that at least one of the guards had survived. He asked his men to find Igor and bring the soldier to his tent.

As soon as Igor was told that Captain Mikalovitch wanted to see him, he knew he was in serious trouble. It would be difficult for him to pretend to have been guarding when there were men who could vouch that he'd been fast asleep in bed the whole time. If he tried to make up a story, he might get confused in some details or someone else might contradict him. As Igor approached the captain's quarters, he decided that his only was out was to tell a horrible lie.

When he entered the captain's tent, his commander looked at Igor fiercely and demanded, "Igor, why didn't you warn us earlier? Don't you know that the penalty for sleeping at one's post is death? Could it be that you were dozing and were unaware of the approaching army till it was too late?"

Igor stared directly into the captain's face and replied, "Captain, I've been wanting to tell you this for a very long time. I decided to wait until I had more proof before letting you know what I suspected. Unfortunately, not only were my suspicions true, but we suffered great losses because of them. How I wish I had been quicker to advise you!

"Do you remember, Captain," he went on, "when Sergei first carried that young boy, Dimitri, into the camp? He told us he had found him by the side of the road, nearly dead. I always wondered what that boy was doing by the roadside. Where did he come from? It never made sense to me, but every time I asked Sergei about it, he told me he didn't want to pressure Dimitri for information. Sergei said that Dimitri must have gone through hard times, and it was a part of his life he wanted to forget. It made me suspect that perhaps it wasn't a coincidence that Sergei found the boy there at that spot."

Igor stared brazenly into the face of Captain Mikalovitch. "For many months the Russian army has been trying to locate our rebel base. I believe they planted Dimitri there as a government spy."

Fueled by his own lies, Igor continued, "You are a great captain. You found us a place to hide where we could stay forever. But we are a thorn in the side of the Russian army. Dimitri was planted by the roadside so we would find him and bring him here. Then he alerted the authorities. They couldn't find us on their own, but with this boy..."

Igor's voice trailed off, and he gave Captain Mikalovitch a few moments to absorb this information. Then he drew a quick breath and continued.

"I've always kept a close eye on Dimitri. Certain things about him don't seem to make sense. Where are Dimitri's parents? Where are his friends? Why, after being brought to the base and recovering here, didn't he want to leave us and go home? Why has he been here all this time?

"Are you beginning to see what I see, Captain? I thought about it long and hard. A week ago I came up with a plan to prove my suspicions. I will be very honest with you. Just a few days ago, I asked Dimitri if he would do guard duty instead of me for just one night. I was pretty sure he would refuse. Who wants to spend the night standing in the cold instead of sleeping?"

By this time Igor had become very bold. His face was flushed, and his anger seemed genuine to Captain Mikalovitch. "Go on," said the captain in a firm voice. His expression was grim.

Igor's voice quickened. His face became red, and sweat started dripping down his neck.

"Dimitri jumped at the chance to do guard duty!" Igor declared. "He was all too eager to take my place. Of course, I didn't really allow him to take my place. I pretended to go back to my tent to get some sleep, but I was never more than fifty yards away from Dimitri the whole night. He didn't know I was there, but I never took my eyes off him.

"Twice during the night Dimitri left his post for over half an hour. Each time he headed away from the camp. I was afraid to follow him because I didn't want to leave our camp unguarded. I thought he might be making contact with the other side. But I wasn't sure, so I said nothing to you."

The captain sighed. Somehow Igor's words didn't ring true. But the captain was tired and hungry and in pain from his wounds. All he wanted was to go to sleep.

"Last night," said Igor earnestly, his voice dropping, "when my turn to guard came around again, Dimitri approached me. Believe it or not, he asked if he could take my place again. I didn't think anything would happen, so I agreed, knowing I'd be nearby the whole time."

The captain was getting impatient. "Get to the point, Igor!"

Igor's voice dropped even lower. In a confidential tone

he related the rest of his story.

"I was watching as carefully as I could, not more than twenty feet away from Dimitri. He started running from the base. It only took a second for me to realize that something very strange was going on. I had no idea that the other two guards were dead by that time, but I did know that trouble was brewing.

"Before I knew it, I saw movement in the distance." Igor paused a moment for effect. "This was the moment we hoped would never come. I shot my gun into the air as a warning to the camp. I believe many lives were saved because of this. I didn't realize the danger earlier because the government forces were so well camouflaged. But as soon as they started approaching, I reacted quickly."

The captain's eyes were beginning to close, but he forced himself to stay awake. *Igor's probably right*, he thought. He could no longer think clearly and just wanted to get the whole business over with.

Seeing signs of the captain's fatigue, Igor realized he'd better talk faster. "By now I knew Dimitri was a spy, but it was too late. I did everything I could to defend our camp. I was about to come to you when you sent for me. I wanted to tell you firsthand about this vicious betrayal by a boy we've treated so well these past few months."

Igor sighed. "Well, Captain, that's my story. I was there when all this happened. I would never desert my post. I hope you'll realize that my intentions were good and that I did save many lives by my warning."

Captain Mikalovitch stared at Igor in silence. He hadn't been expecting this long story when he'd called for the soldier. But the more he considered it, the more he thought it could be true. Igor, of course, would never leave his post. He was a loyal soldier, devoted to the rebel cause. What's more, Igor had warned everybody of the attack. It made him angry to think he'd been harboring a spy at his secret base. He couldn't believe he hadn't seen through Dimitri himself. How could he have been fooled all these months by the boy's sweet nature? Now the captain knew what had been happening all along. Dimitri had been so nice only to trick him and everyone else into thinking he was just an innocent boy.

Captain Mikalovitch had lost forty-two soldiers, all of them good men. He needed somebody to blame for this tragedy, and now that person had been found. Dimitri was the culprit. The boy wasn't going to get away with this! He would make an example out of Dimitri and hang him in public for being a traitor.

While Captain Mikalovitch thought all this over in his head, Igor couldn't figure out whether he had been caught in his web of lies or whether his story had been accepted as fact. He was relieved when the captain finally spoke.

"Igor, thank you," said the captain at last. "You're a real hero, and you'll be well rewarded for your efforts. Bring Dimitri to me. We'll throw him in jail and prepare him for his punishment. Thank you for making me aware of what I should have figured out by myself long ago."

Igor left with a big smile on his face. How easily he'd

gotten away with it! How wonderfully all the details fit! His life was saved. If Dimitri had to die, so be it.

On his way to find the boy, Igor ran into Sergei. "Where's Dimitri?" More than anyone else, he probably knew where the boy was.

Sergei saw a look in Igor's eyes that he didn't like. Suspiciously he asked, "What do you need Dimitri for?" When Igor began to explain, Sergei interrupted him. "Why does the captain want Dimitri?"

Igor answered shamelessly, "Don't you remember who was standing guard at the time? It was supposed to be me, but it was Dimitri. Don't you realize I could be sentenced to death for not being at my post?"

The air seemed suddenly still. Not a bird sang, not a leaf rustled. Sergei looked at Igor in shock. "I wonder if the captain knows this."

Igor said, "Well, not only did he realize that I was supposed to be there, but he now knows that Dimitri is a spy. You'll hear the whole story at the hanging."

"The hanging?" Sergei stared at Igor in utter disbelief. "Are you crazy? Dimitri, a spy? Come on, Igor, you know better than that. He wouldn't know how to spy if he tried."

Igor answered coldly, "That's not my concern. You don't want me to give up my life for some little boy, do you? Come on, tell me where he is."

"I don't know," said Sergei. "Do you think I follow him around all day? What Dimitri does and where he goes is his business."

Sergei was stalling. Of course he knew where Dimitri was; he looked after him all the time.

"Come to think of it, Igor," he went on, "I think I saw him walk toward the kitchen. Yes, I remember now. He said he'd be peeling potatoes this afternoon."

Without another word, Igor turned on his heel and headed toward the kitchen. The second he was gone, Sergei ran to the makeshift tent where Dimitri was sleeping.

"Dimitri, wake up. They think you're a spy, and they're blaming you for the ambush and the soldiers who were killed!

"Take my rifle and my knife. And here's a canteen of water. Run as fast as you can. If they catch you, you'll be put to death. Run, Dimitri!"

Dovid could hardly believe his ears. If anything, he had saved people's lives. Why was he being blamed? But he knew he could trust Sergei. Sergei had saved his life, carrying him to the camp on his shoulder. If Sergei told him to leave, he had to leave.

They hugged each other like true brothers, and Sergei wept. "Dimitri," he said, "there is no time to lose. Run, my friend. Escape!"

Tears streamed down Dovid's face. "Thank you for everything, Sergei. I will not forget you!"

"Go that way," said Sergei, pointing to a certain path. "They'll never look for you there."

Their eyes locked one last time, then Dovid turned and was gone.

ON THE RUN

Sergei went back to his tent and lay down, waiting for the worst. Igor had looked all over the camp, but the boy could not be found. It didn't take him long to realize that Dimitri had escaped. Immediately, Igor ran to the captain.

"Dimitri's gone!"

Captain Mikalovitch swore in anger and frustration. "Quickly, pull together a group of men. You'll head the search party. I want Dimitri back. I can't let a spy escape!

"There's only one way he could have gone. You're experienced soldiers, and he's just a young boy. Get moving. Now!"

Igor got moving. With five soldiers under his command, he took off into the forest.

Igor wanted to find Dimitri quickly so he could be back at camp before nightfall. He was exhausted from the battle, the lies — the whole nasty business. But if Igor's interest was half-hearted, Dimitri was running for his life. He knew they had more experience tracking in the bushes than he had in escaping.

Dovid was terrified, but his terror made him run all the faster. The adrenaline rushed through his body and pushed him on.

After running for some time, Dovid came to a fork in the path. He took a few seconds to stop and catch his breath. Where to go next? Should he run to the left or right? Making a quick decision, he turned left and continued racing as fast as he could, pausing every now and then to take a quick drink of water.

Dovid made good time as he distanced himself from the army camp. But Igor and his men were highly trained. They quickly made up some of the distance that separated them from Dovid and soon reached the fork in the road. Igor, with five soldiers helping him, would be able to cover both paths.

He yelled out his orders. "Three of you turn right. I'll head to the left with the others. In an hour you should know if you're on the right track. If not, head back here. We'll meet again at this fork in the road. Do your best to catch that little monster!"

Igor ran with his fellow soldiers in the direction Dovid had gone. After a while, Dovid could hear their footsteps and the sound of shouting voices. He knew he did not have long before they'd catch up to him.

Thinking furiously, Dovid came up with a dangerous plan. As he ran, he watched for a tree whose branches hung over the path. After running only a few minutes, he found exactly what he was looking for. One of the branches appeared strong enough to carry his weight, and he quickly climbed the tree until he was ten feet above ground. He didn't think his pursuers would bother looking up if they were checking for tracks on the ground.

And so it was. A few minutes later, Igor and his companions ran right under Dovid's perch in hot pursuit. Sighing with relief, Dovid leaned back against the trunk. He'd stay up there for a while to make sure they were truly gone.

Dovid stayed up in the tree for hours. Soon night fell, and he longed for rest. But he had to move on. He had to get away. He climbed down and began to make his way through the forest in the dark. He had no idea if he was heading in the right direction. Perhaps, instead of running away from the camp, he was circling toward it.

Soon Dovid could not go on anymore. He needed to sleep. He found shelter beneath a tree, whose hanging branches fell almost to the forest floor. He gathered up some leaves and grasses and covered himself. He would be safe there, hidden from anyone passing by.

Grateful for the food and water Sergei had given him, Dovid ate a quick, if meager, supper. Then he fell into a deep sleep.

After what seemed like a few minutes, Dovid was awakened by the feel of cold, hard metal jabbing at his neck. A voice said loudly, "One move and you're dead, kid."

Dovid lay there silently, not even turning his head to see

who was standing over him.

He heard the man call out, "Hey, you guys, get some rope and tie him up. I should kill him on the spot, but the general probably wants to talk to him before we finish him off. Make sure the ropes are tight so he can't escape."

Dovid's hands were tightly bound, and a blindfold was put over his eyes. He was yanked to his feet and told to start walking. Dovid walked clumsily, achy from being in a cramped space for so long. He begged to be allowed to speak.

"Save your words for the general, traitor," said the man roughly.

Then it dawned on Dovid what had transpired. He was dressed in the uniform of the rebel army. Anyone seeing him would naturally assume that he was a rebel soldier. Why should they think he was just a boy, a civilian wearing army clothes only because he didn't have clothes of his own? In silence, he trudged on.

After a long, hard march they reached the army base. Dovid was taken to a small cabin and dumped roughly on the hard wooden floor. After what seemed like hours, the door opened. He was pulled to his feet and half dragged to another location a short distance away. At this point the blindfold was removed, and he stood face-to-face with a general of the Russian army.

The man was tall and well built. He had thick, wavy dark hair streaked with gray, and his black eyes were commanding.

"I'm General Petrovitch," he told Dovid, "and you are our prisoner." Surprisingly, the general spoke in a reasonable voice, but there was a menacing air to his every word.

After looking Dovid over, the general remarked, "They're really picking their soldiers young these days. You can't be more than, say, fifteen or sixteen years old. The rebels must be losing this war if they have to enlist children your age."

The general paused and stared at Dovid, as if considering what to do with him. "What's your name, boy?" he barked.

"My name is Dimitri," replied Dovid. "And whatever you're thinking about me, you're wrong. Please let me explain. I'm not a rebel soldier at all."

General Petrovitch looked at him in surprise. "Well," he said, "you certainly could have fooled me with that uniform."

Dovid pleaded with the general. "Please, sir, just give me a chance to explain."

The general glanced at his time piece and said, "I have a little time before my next meeting. What do you have to say for yourself?"

As quickly and earnestly as possible, Dovid started talking. He related everything that had happened from the time Sergei found him in the woods. He swore he was not a rebel soldier; in fact, the rebels were trying to kill him.

Dovid's voice was as sincere as he could make it. As he continued with his story, the general appeared to be listening more closely. Although the story seemed outlandish, General Petrovitch sensed there was truth in the boy's words. He started asking him questions to see whether he would change the details as he went along. The general tried to trip him up several times, but everything seemed to add up. Finally the general came to a decision.

"Young man," he said to Dovid, "your story is preposterous. On the other hand, it's so strange it could actually be true. I am a fair and decent man, and I don't want to kill an innocent person. But what should I do with you? If you are lying and really are a rebel soldier, I can't let you go."

Dovid jumped in quickly. "Please, General Petrovitch! Everything I've told you is true. Let me join your army. I know how to shoot a gun. I know how to use a knife. I've been living with soldiers for the past several months. I'll do any work you give me without complaint. I have nowhere to go, and the only life I know now is army life."

General Petrovitch considered his request. If the boy really was a rebel soldier, this would be an ideal way for him to spy and relay everything he learned to his friends. On the other hand, he was only a boy, after all. And if he really knew all those things, he might make a good Russian soldier one day.

The general decided to let Dovid stay for the time being. He ordered the soldier who'd brought him in to find him a bed and some clothes. Grateful, Dovid left without a word.

As soon as Dovid left, General Petrovitch asked for Grigory, one of his most trusted soldiers. When he came, he told him the whole story. It was decided that Dovid would be part of Grigory's group and that Grigory would keep a close eye on him. The general told Grigory that chances were the boy was innocent, but he added, "If you notice anything out of the ordinary, if you see the boy leave the camp even for a moment, if anything strikes you as suspicious, you have my permission to kill him on the spot."

Grigory nodded in agreement. "Don't worry, sir. I'll watch him every second and let you know if there's anything suspicious."

And so Dovid started his life as a soldier in the Russian army.

RETURN TO RUKICHKI

The town of Rukichki, where Dovid had grown up, had seen many changes in his absence. There was great turmoil within Russia, but for more than ten years the townspeople led quiet lives, hardly caring about the social unrest that surrounded them. Rabbi Silverberg led his congregation wisely, stressing Torah values and overcoming the lust for money that ruled the lives of so many of their neighbors.

About twelve years after the incident with Dovid, a new tragedy gripped the small town. The mayor of Rukichki died.

Throughout Russia, every mayor had undisputed power over his village and ruled with an iron hand. A mayor could even decide matters of life and death. Luckily for the Jews of Rukichki, the old mayor, Oleg Nikolaevitch, had been kind and reasonable. During the many years he had been in power, he had ruled with absolute fairness. When tax increases were announced, everyone, Jew and non-Jew alike, was taxed the same. The Jews were treated no different from anybody else — quite unusual in czarist Russia.

The Jewish population of Rukichki were grateful for this, for they knew that in many of the surrounding towns life was much harder. This was particularly true in the next province, Vitbesk. There the Jews of Dubena and Arsenova were ruled by mayors who were incredibly cruel. In certain towns, the Jewish community was forced to pay outrageous taxes. For whenever the mayor of a town needed extra money, there was an easy solution — tax the Jews more.

Now that Oleg Nikolaevitch lay dead, everyone was afraid that the new mayor might not be so easygoing. Perhaps their years of peace were over. Perhaps now they would be treated like the Jews in the next town, always wondering when the next terrible blow would fall. They could even be forced to leave.

The Jewish community lived with this fear for many months. Then, one day, it was announced that the new mayor would be arriving shortly. They had never heard of Mayor Dimitri, and everyone was very nervous. Even the gentiles wanted to make a good impression.

Both groups organized welcoming parties in honor of the new mayor. In the non-Jewish part of town, all the buildings were repainted and the streets repaired. The walls were scrubbed, and the public squares were thoroughly cleaned. Large signs were displayed all over, announcing, "WELCOME, MAYOR DIMITRI."

In the Jewish section, similar preparations were underway. The Jews worked doubly hard to impress the new mayor. It was decided that all the children would gather and present him with flowers as he entered the city. Lavish gifts were also purchased for him. Music would be played. Choirs would sing. Children would dance. It would be a day the townspeople would never forget.

The much feared, much anticipated day finally arrived, and a big red carpet was set up in the city square. At two o'clock, a carriage appeared in the distance. Four horsemen led the procession, and another four followed behind. Within a few minutes, the crowd could clearly discern that the eight horsemen were all dressed in black from head to toe. There were black horses leading the carriage, and the entire impression was one of darkness and foreboding. A feeling of unease pervaded the air, and everyone was still. There was not a sound to be heard, even from the children.

The carriage stopped in the square. The mayor could be seen through the windows of the carriage, but he did not come out to greet the people. There was no word from the mayor, so the gentile presentation began. A choir sang and a band played. Everyone made an attempt to put on a brave face, but the atmosphere was strained. Finally, with the presentation of a golden cup to the mayor, the ice was broken and people began to relax. Everybody shouted, "Welcome, Mayor Dimitri!" and it was obvious from the smile on his face that the mayor was pleased.

There was one thing that worried the people. The

mayor appeared to be very young, no more than twenty-five years old. The townspeople could not be sure if the mayor's youth would work in their favor or not.

Soon the presentations were over in the gentile part of town. One of the non-Jewish leaders told the mayor that although the Jewish community comprised just over fifty families, they, too, wanted to formally welcome him. So the mayor and his entourage made their way to the Jewish area.

As Mayor Dimitri approached, fear struck deep into the heart of every Jew. The fearful appearance of the guards gave everyone a sense of helplessness and desperation. Why had the mayor brought these men with him? There was already a police force in town. What was the mayor going to do? What changes would take place?

The mayor's carriage came to a stop, and, as in the gentile section, he and his entourage remained silent. After an awkward moment, the children took the initiative and stepped forward to offer their flowers. Four elderly, distinguished members of the community approached with the Jewish people's gift. Of course, they couldn't spend the same amount of money as the larger gentile population, but they had managed to purchase a silver snuffbox for the mayor.

As soon as he was handed the snuffbox, the mayor took one look at it and threw it to the ground. Then he started screaming, "You think you can pacify me with a snuffbox? No gift in this world can buy me off, and I know that's what you're trying to do!"

Everyone gasped in shock. Mayor Dimitri stared at

them long and hard. "Doesn't anyone recognize me?" he demanded.

What was the mayor talking about? How could they recognize him when they had never seen him before?

Finally the mayor spat out in anger, "I am Dovid, the boy you persecuted so cruelly twelve years ago. I've been looking forward to this day for a long time. Do you think I've forgotten how you accused me of robbery and drove me away? I was only fourteen years old! Just a year past my bar mitzvah!"

In spite of himself, Dovid turned his head, tears brimming in his eyes. Quickly, he regained his composure and faced the townspeople with renewed fury.

"How could you accuse me of robberies I did not commit? Would I rob the people who had taken me in? To this day I remember vividly the moment Rabbi Silverberg came to my bedroom and accused me of stealing the letter opener. How it got into my trunk I will never know. Someone planted it there! I never took it! I never took anything!

"You people didn't want me. You didn't want my sister. You got rid of her easily by sending her to relatives in the next town. And me? You plotted against me!"

The crowd gasped. They could not believe what they were hearing.

"I will not rest, " swore Dovid, "until I take revenge on every single one of you! I am not poor little Dovid anymore. I am Mayor Dimitri, and I can do with you whatever I want.

"Tomorrow morning there will be new rules posted. And

if you're wondering why these eight men are with me, the answer is simple. They're my private police force. Because of the new rules I'm instituting, I'm going to need a little more manpower. My private police force will not stand for any nonsense. They'll make sure that whatever I command will be obeyed."

The Jews were in very serious trouble. What could possibly be in store for them now? They quickly dispersed and returned to their homes.

No one in the Jewish community slept well that night. Their peaceful existence of the past twenty years had come to an end. They wondered what the new mayor would demand from them. Would the taxes be raised? Would they be physically harassed? Would they be driven into exile? No one knew.

Early the next morning everyone was in the streets, watching the mayor's private guards post signs. There were many rules, one more terrible than the next. Jews would not be allowed to leave the city without permission from the mayor. Jews would not be allowed to do business in the gentile part of town without permission from the mayor. If a Jew passed by a church, he must bow his head in respect. Any Jew who passed a gentile in the street would have to bid him "good morning" and show him honor by bowing his head.

The final edict was the most cruel. Every single Jew in the community would have to pay two thousand rubles for the privilege of remaining in the town. Written below this statement was the following: "If there be any Jew, man, woman, or child, who does not fulfill this requirement within forty-eight hours, he or she will be thrown into jail to await the death penalty."

The community was thrown into a panic. The other rules were bad enough, but how could they raise two thousand rubles for each family member? They were poor people to begin with. They hardly had enough money to stay alive. And they had only forty-eight hours to find an answer!

THE HOSTAGE

The Jews of Rukichki called an emergency meeting. One person urged that they leave town and move to a friendlier place. But the rules stated that any Jew wishing to leave town could take with him only one suitcase. His business, his house, and whatever he owned would belong to the mayor. What would they do without their livelihoods?

One man pointed out, "We all know the troubles that have befallen our Jewish brothers elsewhere. Who says that after we move the same thing won't happen in the new place? We really have no choice!"

So the Jews decided to do everything they could to raise the money. Some went to relatives and asked them for loans; others sold precious family heirlooms. Some even sold their clothing and furniture. Others were forced to sit on the side of the road begging.

Unbelievably, within forty-eight hours all the money

was collected. People had lost their prized possessions and taken out large loans, but now the people of the town would be allowed to stay.

Only one family was unable to come up with the money: the Silverbergs. The daughter of the rabbi, Rifkah, whose husband had been killed not long after the untimely death of Dovid's parents, had raised her young family in her parents' house. She had been left with three children: twin boys, Hershel and Yitzchak, age fourteen, and Sarah, eighteen. Rifkah, like her parents, sold everything she owned but could raise only eight and a half thousand rubles. When she brought the money to the mayor's office, she enclosed a letter promising to pay the rest within a few weeks. Her father, Rabbi Silverberg, even offered to work for the city for free in order to pay off the debt.

The mayor read Rabbi Silverberg's letter and laughed. He was not going to be swayed by such silliness. Right away he called for four of his policemen.

"Go to the Silverbergs' house," he ordered, "and seize the girl, Sarah. Throw her in prison. I'll decide what to do with her later."

In the small Jewish quarter, everyone heard the sound of the carriage. The horses' footfalls clattered against the cobblestones as the mayor's men rode by. No one was surprised when the carriage stopped in front of the Silverberg house. They were going to take the rabbi away, that was for sure!

The soldiers began pounding on the door, shouting, "If

you don't open the door this minute, we'll smash it down."

When Rifkah opened the door, the men rushed in and knocked her down. She was not important to them — they had come for her daughter, Sarah.

Rabbi Silverberg, hearing the commotion, told his grandsons and grandaughter to hide under their beds. Meanwhile, the policemen ransacked the house. "Where is the girl, Sarah? She's the one we want. Hand her over right now!"

Rabbi Silverberg shouted, "No, don't take her! She's not to blame! Please, leave my granddaughter alone! Take me instead."

The thugs ignored him and continued their search. It didn't take them long to find Sarah and drag her, kicking and screaming, from her bedroom. They yanked her through the front door and threw her into the carriage.

The Silverbergs wept as the mayor's men pulled away with Sarah inside the carriage. She was thrown into a dark cell. The door was bolted, and Sarah was completely alone.

She lay there in the dark, crying for her mother and grandfather, terrified of what her fate would be. Finally, exhausted and utterly worn out, she fell into a fitful sleep.

It was late at night, but people started pouring into the streets, headed for the Silverbergs. Everybody wept. After all, the sign had said "death penalty." The mayor would put their rabbi's granddaughter to death because they were short fifteen hundred rubles. Terror filled the heart of every Jew, and the Silverberg family could not be consoled.

Within an hour, a delegation appeared at Mayor Dimitri's office, begging for Sarah's release. Two policemen stopped them at the door and demanded that they leave at once. When the Jews insisted that they see the mayor immediately, the policemen laughed and told them they'd be arrested if they didn't go home.

Just then, Mayor Dimitri opened a window and yelled, "What do they want? Let them in."

In a moment, the men stood in the presence of Mayor Dimitri. They begged him to release Sarah and promised that all the money would be in his hands by the following morning.

Mayor Dimitri said to them, "This is only the beginning of my rule in this town. No one should think I have less mercy than you. The girl stays in the prison tonight. However, if the money is in my office by nine o'clock tomorrow morning, I'll let her go. If not, she'll be dead by ten."

The men thanked Mayor Dimitri profusely and rushed off to let the Silverbergs know what was happening. Everyone in the community went looking for spare change. Money that had been set aside for food, for the children's milk, for other important purposes, was collected and brought to the Silverberg house.

Slowly most of the money was collected, but still there was not enough. A number of people volunteered to go on horseback to neighboring towns to collect money from family and friends, and they returned before dawn with a significant amount.

The Hostage

By nine o'clock in the morning, the money was ready. There was barely a penny left in any Jewish home, but at least Sarah would be freed.

True to his word, Mayor Dimitri let Sarah go. She ran from the cell into the arms of her mother, sobbing with relief.

Still, the people were afraid. What if Mayor Dimitri imposed another tax? They surely could not do this again!

A man named Yossi had an idea. "Listen, everybody," he said, "I remember when Dovid lived in our town. I'm about his age, and we were in the same class at school. We played together all the time. Perhaps if I, and a few other schoolmates, were to meet with Dovid and try to talk to him about old times, he'd take pity on us."

Many of those present nodded in approval. Anything was worth a try.

That afternoon, Yossi and three other young men turned up at Mayor Dimitri's office. This time, when the policemen stopped them at the door, Yossi spoke up. "I'm sure Mayor Dimitri would like to see us. I am his friend from school. Tell him Yossi is here to see him."

The policemen smirked in disdain, anticipating the quick refusal they were sure Yossi was about to receive. To their surprise, Mayor Dimitri agreed to see them, and the young men walked into his office.

Yossi stuck out his hand with a smile and said, "Hi, Dovid. Do you remember us?"

Mayor Dimitri looked at him with a cold eye and did not stretch out his hand. "What if I do remember you? What do you want from me?"

Yossi said, "Please, Mayor Dimitri. Do you remember the time we went swimming in the river together, and it began to rain, and our clothes got soaked? We got into so much trouble together!"

Yossi's efforts to be friendly and effusive didn't work. No smile lit up the face of Mayor Dimitri.

The mayor retorted, "You can have pleasant memories of this town. You grew up here and were allowed to stay. I can only remember being forced to go away. I was accused of being a thief. No one showed me any mercy. That is my only memory of this 'wonderful' town!"

Dovid's voice grew louder as he spoke, and he banged on the table. His face was flushed. "Now," he said angrily, "leave before it is too late. Revenge is the only thing I want."

Yossi and his friends retreated in disappointment. They had accomplished nothing.

THE INSPECTION

The very next night new signs went up in town. This time it was from the chief health inspector. Of course, the chief health inspector was Mayor Dimitri. He was now the chief of everything. The signs indicated that there would be an inspection of every store in town the following week. Mayor Dimitri himself would lead the inspection team. He would check to see that all the stores in the city upheld the proper laws which he listed on the signs. He would be searching for any breach of health or safety regulations. The signs noted that the inspections could start as early as the following morning, and any store that did not pass would be closed down indefinitely.

Every Jewish store owner was extremely worried. Was this only an excuse to close them down? They could not take a chance, so every shopkeeper, along with his relatives and friends, stayed up all night scrubbing every inch of his store well beyond the requirements. If everything were perfect, they hoped, Mayor Dimitri would have no reason to close them down. But their hope was in vain.

The next morning, at ten o'clock, Mayor Dimitri and his policemen appeared in the Jewish section of town. People wondered whether he would even bother inspecting stores owned by gentiles.

His first stop was the Kellers' fish store. Mayor Dimitri had a bright smile on his face as he addressed Mr. Keller. "Good morning, Mr. Keller. I am here for an official inspection. If you pass, everything will be fine. But if this store isn't clean enough, you realize, of course, that I will have to close it down."

Mr. Keller smiled outwardly but was trembling inside. The mayor walked up and down the aisles searching for dirt, dust, or other signs of uncleanliness, but he found nothing.

Mr. Keller was beginning to breathe a little more easily. When it appeared that the inspection was about to end, Mayor Dimitri called two of his policemen. "Bring me a ladder," he demanded. "There is still plenty to check out in this store."

The policemen brought him a ladder and set it against one of the walls. Mayor Dimitri climbed up into the rafters and took out a brand-new, perfectly white glove from his pocket and put it on. He rubbed a gloved finger against one of the wooden rafters. With a big smile on his face, he yelled, "Look, my glove is dirty! This store is a mess! How could anyone eat food that comes from here?"

Mayor Dimitri signaled to his men. "Put up a sign outside that this store is closed until further notice," he bellowed. "I must protect the citizens of my town from any health hazard." Then he made his way down the road to the next store.

By this time, those who had seen what happened to the Kellers had run to warn the next storekeeper. In the ten minutes it took the mayor to arrive at Moishe's grocery, six men had climbed up to the rafters with buckets of soap and water and wiped away all signs of dirt and dust. They were sure Mayor Dimitri would be unable to find any reason to close down the store.

Mayor Dimitri made a grand entrance. He informed Moishe that he was on official business. "Listen, Jew. Obviously you want to keep a clean store. You shouldn't be worried about my inspection. Let's get on with it."

The mayor walked through Moishe's store and could find nothing wrong. Then, with a twisted smile, he called for his policemen once again and asked them to bring a ladder. He was sure he'd find dust in the rafters and be able to destroy Moishe's business as he had destroyed the Kellers'.

Mayor Dimitri's goons set up the ladder at the back of the store, and he climbed up to the highest beams. But this time he was in for a surprise. His glove was still clean after he'd made his inspection. The mayor tried again, and yet a third time, with no success. He finally realized that all the beams were perfectly clean.

Mayor Dimitri scowled — he did not like to be outsmarted. But while his policemen were taking the ladder back outdoors, a fly took advantage of the open doorway and entered the premises.

"What?" shouted the mayor. "You allow flies in your store? Don't you know what a hazard that is to public health? Guards, close down this store for at least two weeks till it is rid of this infestation. We'll see about reopening at our second inspection."

Moishe, the owner, said in consternation, "But, Mayor, that fly only came in a few seconds ago! If your men hadn't opened the door, the fly would never had gotten in."

Mayor Dimitri laughed in Moishe's face. "I don't need your excuses. I want absolute cleanliness, and your store doesn't pass my rigid test. I will return in two weeks for another inspection."

Now the other Jews in the community knew what to expect. Mayor Dimitri continued down the street, and Goldberg's Butcher Shop was next on his list. Mr. Goldberg's friends had already started cleaning every wall and every wooden surface in his store, including the rafters. Several other people stood at the entrance to his store with fly swatters. Woe to any fly or other insect that would try to enter that shop!

The mayor tried the white-glove test but failed to come up with even a speck of dirt. Next he searched for flies and vermin and had his men keep the door open throughout the inspection in the hope that a fly would enter. Once or twice it appeared as if he would be successful, but the men outside swatted the flies that hovered around the doorway before

The Inspection 119

they were able to enter the store.

It seemed that this time Mayor Dimitri would not succeed. "Well, Mr. Goldberg," he said, "I must admit that this store does meet my requirements for cleanliness. Every beam is perfectly clean, and there are no insects on the premises. In fact, I'm so impressed with the way you maintain your store that I have decided to start shopping here."

At this, Mr. Goldberg thought to himself, *Maybe Mayor Dimitri is not as bad as everyone says. He recognizes a clean store when he sees one. He's even willing to shop here. Who says he doesn't like Jews?*

With a smile, Mr. Goldberg turned to the mayor and said, "My dear Mayor Dimitri, I am at your service. Tell me what you would like."

Mayor Dimitri carefully inspected all the meats for sale and selected many different cuts. He practically emptied the store.

Mr. Goldberg was incredibly excited. In his head a flashing cash register was adding up how much money Mayor Dimitri was spending. What vast profits Mr. Goldberg would earn!

When everything was all wrapped up, Mr. Goldberg wrote out a long bill, itemizing each purchase, and handed it to the mayor.

Mayor Dimitri looked at him in astonishment. "Goldberg, you think I should pay for this food? I am doing you a favor just by using your products. Whoever hears that Mayor Dimitri purchases his meat at this butcher shop will shop here, too. And you expect me to pay for bringing you business? How ungrateful can you be? How dare you insult me by presenting me with a bill?" The mayor crumpled up the bill and threw it on the floor.

Mr. Goldberg realized then that he was ruined as a butcher. He had lost more than half his meat without receiving even a penny for it. There was no way he could restock his store without the money he should have received for the meat. He was in even worse shape than the first two shopkeepers — at least they still had all their merchandise.

Mr. Goldberg, a man of advanced years, began to weep. He begged Mayor Dimitri to pay him. The mayor gave a cruel laugh as his men took his packages and left the store. It seemed there would be no end to the tortures he had in store for the Jews of the town where he'd grown up. His revenge was bitter.

THE MAKINGS OF A MAYOR

how did Mayor Dimitri come to be the mayor of this town? How could he, after leaving town at fourteen, return as mayor at twenty-six?

After he'd been accepted into the Russian army, Dovid had been assigned to a certain unit. To make sure he wasn't a spy, he was always under the watchful eye of a superior officer.

Dovid was happy to be in the army. It was a life he had become used to. One day when the captain, whose name was Ivanovitch, asked for volunteers for a very dangerous mission, ten men stepped forward. Dovid was among them.

The captain was surprised when he saw the young boy among the volunteers. "Sorry, Dimitri, this is not a job for a boy of your age. Only professional soldiers can handle this."

Dovid begged him for a chance to prove himself. The

captain thought about it. Perhaps he had spoken too hastily. This was a dangerous job where lives were at risk. And who cared if Dimitri lived or died? In the end, Dovid was allowed to join this elite group together with the soldier who was in charge of him.

Dovid was a great help to his division. He did whatever he was ordered to do, no matter how dangerous. It quickly became clear, because of his dedication, that Dovid was on their side. There was no reason to fear he was a rebel spy. Dovid was put on duty just like any other soldier.

In truth, Dovid didn't care if he lived or died. He had no family or friends, and nowhere besides the army to call home. If he died, it would make no difference to anyone. That's why he was brave in the face of battle — braver than any other soldier and willing to take more chances than anyone else.

Before long Dovid's fearlessness in battle became widely known. One day the soldiers went on a particularly dangerous mission. The entire division was sent behind enemy lines to attack a rebel base. Dovid, like every other soldier, was well prepared in advance and knew exactly what he had to do.

Dovid and his fellow soldiers traveled under cover of darkness. They were scheduled to arrive at the enemy camp at midnight. They knew they had more men than the enemy and hoped to destroy the enemy camp and be back at home base by morning.

When they reached the camp, they were in for a very

unpleasant surprise. Their reconnaissance team had given them incorrect information. They'd been told that the rebel camp was small, and that the rebels had run out of rations and were too weak to fight. They'd also been told that there were not enough knives and guns to go around.

When Dovid's division arrived, they sent out new scouts, according to procedure. The news they brought back was bad. In the weeks preceding the army's arrival at the rebel base, reinforcements had arrived. Guns and ammunition were everywhere, and the enemy appeared to be strong and well fed.

Within hours Dovid and the rest of his division were pinned down under heavy fire. The army forces were so heavily outnumbered that they were afraid to stand up in order to retreat. Heavy fire rained on them, and Captain Ivanovitch saw that unless someone could neutralize the soldiers at the point of heavy fire, it was only a matter of time until every man in the division was wiped out.

The captain shouted, "We've got to destroy their artillery. It's our only hope! Who's ready to go in there and do the job?"

Not a soul answered him. They were afraid to look him in the eye for fear that he might take eye contact to mean yes. Only Dovid met his gaze. Only Dovid stepped forward. Only Dovid was ready to go.

"Dimitri, follow me. We'll charge in and attack!"

Dovid and the captain ran toward the enemy lines. Enemy fire was everywhere. Who would live? Who would die in that theater of war?

Captain Ivanovitch and Dovid ran fearlessly through enemy fire toward the main artillery position, shooting as they raced toward their goal. Only a few dozen yards remained. Now the fire was all around them. Bullets buzzed around their heads and grazed their arms. They did not care. They had to destroy the enemy stronghold.

They were almost there. The worst of the gunfire had stopped. During a lull in the shooting, Captain Ivanovitch dashed forward toward the main artillery range. They managed to get some shots in. Under the cover of gunfire the captain quickly lit a branch he had picked up before their charge. He threw it with all his strength, and the building, full of explosive gun powder, exploded. Amid the chaos, Dovid and Captain Ivanovitch were able to make a quick retreat.

They had almost reached their fellow soldiers when disaster struck. "I've been hit in the leg!" cried the captain. His anguished cries rang through the forest.

But it was no use. None of the soldiers hiding among the trees were brave enough to run out across the empty field to save their captain. Sure, they might reach the captain, but then they'd have to lift him up and carry him back to cover right in the line of enemy fire. They wanted to save their captain, but not at the expense of their own lives.

The captain's moans increased. Dovid, who was closest to the wounded officer, decided he was going to try. He knew he might fail, and the captain might die despite his best efforts, but he had to try. The captain had been loyal to him, and Dovid felt he didn't have much to lose. He screamed for the other men to start shooting so he would have some cover to run before the enemy realized what was happening. Then he rushed to the aid of his captain. Miraculously, Dovid reached the captain unhurt. He dragged him by the arms and walked back as quickly as he could to his platoon.

Suddenly Dovid heard a popping sound and felt a thud in his shoulder. Then he heard a scream of pain and anguish from the captain. "They hit me again!"

Ignoring his own pain, Dovid dove to the ground, looking for cover, and ended up behind a large rock. Some of the older soldiers knelt to examine the captain. The second shot had just grazed him — it was only a surface wound. The captain would most likely survive. They dragged him out of range of enemy fire.

When they examined Dovid, they saw that the shot had passed right through his shoulder. Luckily, the bullet had not hit any major artery or limb. He would survive, but he would be in lots of pain. And the wound needed attention to prevent infection.

Since the enemies' main artillery source was destroyed, the soldiers were able to retreat unhurt. After a few yards, they stopped long enough to form makeshift stretchers for the captain and Dovid. A few hours later, they were back at the camp. By now the captain was almost unconscious, but he managed to give the order that Dovid be treated as a hero.

News spread throughout the division that Dovid alone

had gone with the captain, risking his life, to take on the rebels and save the men in his company. They heard how brave he'd been to save the captain's life, even at the cost of getting shot himself.

The story spread throughout all of Russia, from army base to army base. Dovid was given a medal of honor and promoted from private to lieutenant.

Slowly Dovid healed. It was six months before he was able to rejoin his platoon. The captain was in the hospital for a whole year. Eventually they reunited and many times went into battle together with great success.

Word of Dovid's acts of heroism reached the army's highest ranks. Time after time, whenever a commanding officer needed a volunteer, the call went out for the bravest soldier in the Russian army: Dovid.

Many years passed. Dovid seemed to be a good luck charm to those at central command. Whenever he went out to fight, the army forces won. In time he received every medal awarded by the Russian army. By the time he was twenty-six, he had become the youngest general ever to lead a Russian army.

Everybody knew that Dimitri was unlike any other general in the army. Other generals sent their men into battle while they sat in their tents in safety; Dimitri led his soldiers into battle himself. Everyone wanted to serve under him, for they knew that with Dimitri they had the best chance of winning and coming back alive.

The czar of Russia had, of course, heard about the

young hero. He followed his exploits just like everyone else. But Czar Alexander was vaguely unhappy about what he heard. Certainly he was thrilled with Dimitri's military victories. The czar wished all his generals would perform like him. But the czar was a suspicious man, even of his closest advisors. Some of them, he was quite sure, would rejoice at his death. Coups and counter-coups were a way of life in Russia. The czar had to be ever vigilant, always on the lookout for any possible threat to his rule. He was so afraid that he did not even live in the winter palace in St. Petersburg, but ruled from Gatchina, the palace of his great-grandfather Paul I.

Dimitri, a young, devoted general, might seem to hold no threat to anyone else, but the czar thought otherwise. Because of Dimitri's great fame and popular following, he thought he could pose a threat as time went on.

Czar Alexander called in his closest advisers and asked them what they thought. After much discussion, they reached the conclusion that in the future Dimitri might be dangerous. Whoever controls the army controls the country. If, for some reason, Dimitri were to rally his troops in opposition to the czar, there was little doubt where their loyalties would lie. The military would certainly turn from the czar to follow their hero, Dimitri.

The czar worried about this. Dimitri did not appear to have any political ambitions, but that could quickly change. His power and charisma commanded the adoration of the masses as well as the military. This gave him a certain edge over the czar, who was not especially loved by the majority of the Russian population.

One advisor devised a plot to get rid of Dimitri for once and for all. "The simplest solution," he said, "is to have him killed. Next time he goes into battle, one of our own men could simply shoot him. No one would ever guess that he hadn't been hit by an enemy bullet."

The czar sighed. He didn't like the idea. He chose his words carefully. "Dimitri is a hero throughout all of Russia. He is practically a legend. People tell stories about him saving lives, and every schoolchild knows of his bravery in battle."

The next advisor spoke directly and to the point. "Dear and revered czar, while we must get rid of General Dimitri, we can't afford to take the chance of killing him in battle. Somebody might see one of our soldiers shoot him and decide to investigate. It could become public knowledge that it was not the enemy who killed him. Such a plan would easily backfire.

"But I have another solution that could perhaps solve the whole issue quickly and easily. Why don't we find Dovid a position in one of the faraway provinces? Call him to the palace. Tell him he has served Mother Russia so faithfully and so well that you are willing to let him take early retirement and become premier of one of your largest provinces. I'm sure Dimitri would be thrilled with such a reward. Besides, it would be an honorable thing to do in return for his loyal service."

The czar nodded. He wanted to be known as an honorable man.

"Offer him a salary much greater than he's earning now," continued the advisor. "He'll be all too happy to give up his army career. He should be sent far enough away from the capital that he'll be nowhere near the seat of power. Mark my words, honored czar. If you do this, Dimitri will be no trouble at all. There'll be no army for him to lead, so he'll have no followers. Slowly the soldiers will forget their loyalty to him. Then the Russian people will again see you, the czar, as their most revered, supreme master."

Czar Alexander smiled, and the advisor bathed in the glow of his awe and respect. "You, sir," said the czar, "have come up with a brilliant plan. Send for Dimitri immediately."

Within a few days Dovid was at the palace of the czar. He had never seen the czar and knew virtually nothing about him except that he was the czar of all Russia and that he, Dovid, was duty-bound to obey him.

Dovid, who was fearless in the face of enemy fire, was nervous to appear before the czar. In preparation he had dressed in elegant new clothes and cut his hair.

Czar Alexander had a pleasant manner. He had thick, reddish-gold hair and wore a military beard and moustache. The czar greeted Dovid as a national hero. His smile was warm and his handshake firm.

"It's a pleasure to meet you," said the czar. "How are you, Dimitri, my most famous of generals?"

Dovid was overwhelmed by the effusive welcome. Respectfully he replied, "Your Highness, the pleasure is mine. To meet the greatest leader in all of Russian history!"

The czar warmed to this compliment, and from then on, the conversation went very well. The czar told Dovid that since he had served over ten years in the Russian army with great honor and distinction, he deserved a reward. "You will be given the greatest honor that any general has ever received. Right now there are three provinces where a premier is needed. Take your pick. Decide where you'd like to be, and that province is yours to rule as you like. You'll be in charge of everything, and the only person you'll have to report to is me.

"You'll get a very large salary, ten times what you are getting now. You'll live in the greatest palace you could ever imagine. Dozens of servants will be at your beck and call.

"Now," continued the czar decisively, "let's stroll over to the map and figure out where you're going to be posted."

The czar took a pointer from a table, grasped Dimitri's arm, and led him to a huge map of the Russian Empire.

Dovid was not stupid. He knew only army life and was perfectly satisfied with his job, but he understood that the czar was not asking him to take the position. The czar was giving an order. There was no way he could refuse. His life as a soldier was over. No more would he command troops. No more would he lead them into battle.

As the czar pointed out various provinces on the map, Dovid came up with a plan. If he couldn't be a soldier any longer, he knew exactly what he wanted to do.

Deep in the back of his mind burned an ambition he'd been harboring all these years. When he'd become general, he'd put it aside, but the moment the czar gave him the choice, it came back to him with full force. Dovid turned slowly toward the czar. His tone was humble and his words measured.

"Your Highness, how can I thank you for the trust you have placed in me? It is truly an amazing offer. However, I don't think I'm ready to run a whole province. I need to gain some experience first. Maybe I could serve for awhile as mayor of a small town. A few years down the line I'd be able to take over a province. I want to be able to live up to the trust you are placing in me."

The czar looked at him, surprised. "But I'm offering you a much higher position."

Dovid's eyes met those of the czar. "If it's all right with you, Your Highness," he went on, "I have a small request."

The czar was laughing inside. He had no interest at all in having Dimitri become a premier. A small town would suit his needs perfectly. If that's what the young man wanted, then by all means he could have it. Once Dimitri was out of the army and tucked away as mayor of some small town, there'd be little reason to ever advance him.

The czar turned to Dovid and said, "So let's hear your request. Any town or city in particular?"

Dovid sighed, his face flushed with emotion. "There is a small town called Rukichki," he said. "It is barely marked on the map. This is the town I grew up in. It's always been my dream to return as the mayor of that town. I heard that just a few months ago the old mayor died, and he hasn't been replaced yet. If I have to leave the army, could I be appointed mayor of that town instead?"

The czar chuckled to himself. What was the matter with Dimitri? Here he was, being offered a premiership, and all he wanted was to be mayor of some insignificant village. Maybe Dimitri wasn't as smart as everyone said he was.

"Of course, General Dimitri," replied the czar with a smile. "Whatever you want. No problem at all. You'll be posted there within a couple of weeks. You have my blessing."

Dovid was incredibly excited. Before leaving the czar's presence, he asked if it would be possible for him to have six or eight of his trusted soldiers to accompany him as policemen in the town.

"Of course," said the czar, anxious to finish the whole business, "whatever you want."

The czar would have given him much more if Dimitri had only known to ask. With all his courtiers following behind, the czar left with a happy heart. He was getting a great bargain.

Within two weeks, Dovid left with eight soldiers and a magnificent carriage. He also carried with him a great deal of money and was well equipped to take up residence as mayor of his old hometown.

THE PAYBACK

The only factor that motivated Dovid was revenge. During his years in the army he had been occupied with winning battles. He had nearly forgotten how much he hated the Jews of Rukichki. Now that he had the chance to get back at those who had thrown him out, he knew that revenge would be very sweet. He smiled to himself as he thought of what was in store for them.

Mayor Dimitri was duly installed as mayor of the town. As time went on, he proclaimed more and more ordinances against the Jews and gave them little rest.

Shortly before Chanukah, Dovid thought of a new plan to harass the Jews of his town. He remembered the Chanukah of his boyhood. He remembered his parents lighting the menorah. He remembered playing dreidel with his sister. He remembered the gifts and the special foods, the latkes and the doughnuts.

A tear escaped from his eye, but when he realized that

he was becoming sentimental, he pulled himself together. He could not allow himself to get soft. If he did, he would lose control over the townspeople, and then he would be finished. Just as they had been cruel to him, so would he be cruel to them. And Chanukah was a perfect time to set that cruelty upon them.

Harsh new ordinances were proclaimed throughout the Jewish section of Rukichki. First, any Jew putting candles in his window during the eight days of Chanukah would be thrown in jail. Such candles, said Mayor Dimitri, were a fire hazard. As chief fire inspector of the city, the mayor would not put up with such a dangerous practice.

Second, no Jew would be permitted to attend synagogue during the entire eight days. And to avoid even the chance that they would gather elsewhere to celebrate the holiday, he declared that they could not meet even in a private home.

Another rule proclaimed that no more than three Jews could be together at any time during Chanukah unless they were from the same family.

Mayor Dimitri wanted to deprive the Jewish population of all happiness and festivity. He therefore banned the sale of driedels and oil. He also made it clear that no Jew could visit Rabbi Silverberg during the entire eight days of Chanukah. Dovid remembered that many of the rabbi's congregants would visit him during the holiday. They would light Chanukah candles there, sing and dance, eat and enjoy. He also remembered that words of Torah were spoken, and this, he felt, was the most dangerous thing of all. He wanted no threat to his power.

In addition, he blamed the rabbi for all of his suffering as a boy, and he wanted to make him miserable. This year the Jews would not gather at Rabbi Silverberg's house with their platters of food. This year it would not be a happy time — not if Mayor Dimitri could help it.

The mayor's final rule stated that any Jew caught on the streets between eight o'clock at night and six o'clock in the morning would be immediately arrested.

Two young men, Chaim and Yaakov, decided they wouldn't let Mayor Dimitri ruin their Chanukah. They would visit the rabbi no matter what. They would wish him a happy Chanukah, bring him some food, and celebrate with him, even if it meant risking a jail sentence. Although their parents discouraged them, the boys said, "We have nothing to fear. Dimitri can't scare us. We'll go late, when everyone's asleep. We'll blacken our faces and wear dark clothes. That way no one will even be able to see us. There's no way the mayor will find out about our plans."

They were to meet at Chaim's house at midnight, when the streets would be empty. They were sure they would never get caught and were looking forward to bringing joy to the rabbi on this wonderful holiday.

When they were ready to go, they opened the door of Chaim's house and stepped into the street. But as Chaim was about to run across the street, he noticed something. There was a small light burning in the distance, and it seemed to be moving toward them. Someone was approaching with a cigarette dangling from his mouth.

"Who do you think it could be at this time of the night?" asked Chaim.

Yaakov deliberated for a moment. "It must be one of Dimitri's guards," he whispered.

Sure enough, it was. Dimitri had posted guards to make sure the Jews would not have a happy Chanukah. This particular guard was patrolling Chaim's street. There was a second guard right behind him.

Chaim and Yaakov stayed where they were, watching the guards march up and down the street. They saw that it took a minute from the time the guards turned away from the boys to walk to the end of the street. During that time, they could run across without being noticed.

In just a few minutes, their opportunity came. Chaim was to go first. He lowered his head so he would present less of a reflection in the moonlight and started running as quickly as he could. His goal was to reach the garbage can at the edge of the alley.

Just as Chaim reached the garbage can his foot hit a small stone which bumped against the metal of the can. The sound rang clear in the quiet of the night.

Chaim froze in fear. Yaakov waited on the other side of the street to see what would happen.

One guard yelled to the other, "Yuri, did you hear that noise? Something's moving in the alley down there."

Yuri turned toward his partner and said, "I'll check it

out, Ilya. You keep going. If there's anything there, I'll find it."

Yuri started walking toward the spot the noise had come from, the very spot where Chaim was hiding. The boy held his breath and crouched into the shadows. He was relieved when, after a few seconds, Yuri yelled back, "Ilya, it must have been a cat. There's nobody here."

The two soldiers continued their patrol. After a few more minutes Yaakov made his run, and he reached the shelter of the garbage cans unnoticed. From there it was just a short hop across the alleyway. Now they were nearly in front of Rabbi Silverberg's house. All they had to do was dash through the bushes and into the back door of the house.

Again Chaim went first, after determining that no guards were present. It took him only a short time to reach the safety of the bushes. He signaled to Yaakov that the coast was clear. Yaakov followed his friend, and soon they were in the shelter of the bushes.

Suddenly a loud voice boomed, "Aha! So you boys thought you could get to the rabbi's house. Well, I've been waiting here for hours. I knew somebody would try to break the curfew!"

The two boys turned slowly to meet the gaze of Mayor Dimitri.

The mayor called out, "Guards! Grab these Jews!"

Four goons came out of nowhere and grabbed the boys.

"Take these boys to my office. And be quick about it!"

The guards started shoving the boys in the direction of the mayor's office, and their nightsticks came down hard. By the time they reached their destination, Chaim and Yaakov were bruised and bleeding. They were told to sit in a corner, and the guards stood menacingly over them as Mayor Dimitri prepared for some fun.

MIDNIGHT SNACK

"**G**ive me the bags those boys were carrying," Mayor Dimitri barked to his guards. "It's late and I'm hungry from waiting in those bushes. It's time for a midnight snack." He had an evil grin on his face and relished the boys' humiliation.

Mayor Dimitri quickly opened the bags. There he found all the wonderful food that had been prepared for the rabbi in honor of Chanukah. He unwrapped a piece of gefilte fish and started eating it right away.

"Too bad Rabbi Silverberg won't get any of this fish. It's very good. But where is the *chrein*? I'm disappointed, I must say. Whoever prepared this should have sent along some *chrein*. Tell that to your mothers if you ever get out of here alive."

Chuckling, the mayor opened another package. "Strudel! I haven't had a nice Jewish strudel in a long time. Mmm. Very tasty!"

Mayor Dimitri was having great fun. Yaakov and Chaim

sat there in terror, crying in pain from the beatings they'd received, not knowing what would happen next. Suddenly, the door of the mayor's office opened, and a guard entered.

"A Rabbi Silverberg is here to see you," he announced. "Shall I arrest him for breaking the curfew as well?"

"No, no," said Dimitri with a wicked laugh. "Let him in. I'd love to see him."

The rabbi was brought in, and Dimitri gave him a wide, evil smile. "I'm enjoying the delicious food that was made for you, Rabbi. How nice of you to share it with me!" He took out another package. "Um, smells like chicken," he declared. And it was. Chaim's mother's best roast chicken.

The mayor started eating the chicken with obvious enjoyment. Suddenly his face turned red, and he began to choke. He tried to clear his throat, but could not.

Mayor Dimitri was in big trouble. Something was stuck in his throat, and he couldn't cough it up. "Quick," he rasped at the guard, "bring me...a drink."

Water was immediately brought, but it didn't help.

"A piece...of bread...quickly!"

Rabbi Silverberg handed the mayor a piece of challah to push down whatever was stuck in his throat. But this was of no help either.

Mayor Dimitri could hardly breathe and feared he would lose consciousness.

"Doctor...now!" That was all the mayor was capable of saying. He sat there, struggling for his life.

A guard ran out to find a doctor. After only a few minutes, the doctor arrived. By this time Mayor Dimitri had fallen off his chair onto the floor, where he lay choking.

The doctor quickly assessed the situation. He turned Mayor Dimitri over and hit him between the shoulder blades, hoping to dislodge the obstruction. This, too, failed. "Try drinking," the doctor implored. "If it doesn't help, there's one more thing I can try. I can operate and try to remove whatever's in there. But the chance of success isn't great. It's quite likely that you are going to die."

Mayor Dimitri could not believe what he was hearing. He motioned to the rabbi to come closer.

The mayor's face was turning blue. The doctor knew there wasn't much time.

The old man bent his ear toward Mayor Dimitri, and the mayor gasped, "Please...Rabbi, pray to God...to save my life. I still know...that He performs...miracles. I'm dying!"

The rabbi was incredulous. He exclaimed, "What about all the suffering and trouble you've caused the Jews of this community? Why should I pray for your life?"

In an almost inaudible voice, the mayor rasped, "I...swear, Rabbi, that if I am...saved I will...rescind every one of my...laws."

The rabbi was not sure he could believe Mayor Dimitri. "All I can do is pray. Whether Hashem chooses to save you is up to Him."

The mayor's breath was labored. He could hardly be heard. "I...swear to...you. If you...save my life...everything will...change."

Rabbi Silverberg took out the small Tehillim he always carried with him, and he began to pray — not for Mayor Dimitri, but for Dovid, the orphaned Jewish boy. He davened for Dovid, for the souls of Dovid's parents, and for the people of the town who were suffering so much. Meanwhile, the doctor stood by. It was really too late for him to do anything. Whether Mayor Dimitri lived or died was no longer in his hands.

The mayor struggled for breath. It seemed that every breath would be his last. The rabbi continued davening, praying to Hashem to save the life of little Dovid, the boy he remembered with so much love.

Suddenly, with one great cough, the mayor expelled the chicken bone that had been stuck in his throat. The tiny bone lay on the floor like a reproach. A lowly chicken bone had almost taken the life of the mighty Mayor Dimitri!

The mayor inhaled great gulps of air, and his breathing soon became normal once again. He had been saved by the rabbi's prayers and the great *chesed* of Hashem. No one there had any doubt.

Mayor Dimitri shocked everyone with what he had to say. "I am a man of my word. I hereby cancel all the laws I made against the Jews in this town. Guards, pull down all the proclamations that have been posted against the Jews. From now on, they will be treated like all the other citizens.

"Rabbi Silverberg, please take these two boys back to their families, but not until the doctor has had a chance to patch them up. Make sure they have everything they need."

The mayor rose from the floor and walked over to Yaakov and Chaim. "I am very sorry, boys. Very, very sorry. Please forgive me."

Those assembled could not believe what was happening. But the mayor wasn't finished yet.

"Rabbi," he said, turning to Rabbi Silverberg, "I've faced death many times. But this is different. While I was choking and I saw you daven, I remembered..." For a minute the mayor could hardly speak. He took a deep breath and continued. "I remembered...being a Jew. Davening to Hashem. Learning. I thought of my parents and what they would think of me if they could see me today." The tears were flowing now. "I want to do *teshuvah*, to come back to Hashem. I'm sorry for all the suffering I've caused and beg Hashem to forgive me."

"If you are truly sorry, and if you do what you can to make up for the damage you've caused, Hashem will forgive you. I promise," the rabbi said solemnly.

The mayor was silent for a long moment. Then he spoke again. "But how can I ask forgiveness for stealing as a young boy? I truly don't remember doing that."

"Mr. Katz saw you getting out of bed and taking the letter opener," the rabbi said. "I found it in your trunk, yet you acted as shocked at what you'd done as we were."

"It was no act. I really was shocked," Dovid said vehemently. "I thought someone had put those things in my bag to get me in trouble."

"I can't understand it," the rabbi said.

There was silence in the room as the mayor, the rabbi, the doctor, and Chaim and Yaakov tried to figure out what could have happened back then.

Suddenly the doctor spoke up. "Sir," he said with excitement in his voice, "do you know if you ever had a problem with sleepwalking as a child?"

"Sleepwalking?" echoed the mayor in surprise. "Why, yes. I remember my parents telling me that they sometimes found me asleep on the front steps or under a tree in the yard."

"Well, then, that's your answer!" said the doctor with satisfaction. "You must have taken those things in your sleep and were never aware of it. I have heard of cases like this, usually as a result of a sudden loss. In your sleep you were trying to get back something valuable which had been taken from you. In this case, your dear parents."

The mayor looked at the doctor as if a weight had fallen from his heart. His voice was unexpectedly strong as he declared, "I was born a Jew, and I shall die a Jew. Mayor Dimitri is gone forever. From now on," he said with determination, "I will be known as Mayor Dovid."

EPILOGUE

Mayor Dovid was loved by all the people of Rukichki. He treated everyone, Jew and non-Jew alike, with great respect.

The townspeople were sorry for what had happened so many years before, and Dovid forgave them. Before long he was a *ba'al teshuvah* and a *ben Torah*.

There was great rejoicing when Dovid married Sarah Silverberg. Dovid's sister, Devorah, who had married long ago, came all the way from Moscow for the wedding. Indeed, every Jew from miles around came to participate in the *simchah*, and the story of Dovid's return became a touchstone of faith for thousands of people and their descendants.